Mysterious Stone Sites

in the Hudson Valley of New York
and northern New Jersey

Written by
Linda Zimmermann

Eagle Press, New York

Facebook Page for *Mysterious Stone Sites*

https://www.facebook.com/MysteriousHudsonValleyStoneSites

Linda Zimmermann's Facebook Fan Page

http://www.facebook.com/pages/Linda-Zimmermann/116636310250

The author is always looking for sites to explore. If you would like to share a location or find out more about her work:

Write to:

Linda Zimmermann
P.O. Box 192
Blooming Grove, NY 10914

Or send email to:

lindazim@optonline.net

What else is Linda Zimmermann writing? Go to: **www.gotozim.com**

CONTENTS

Acknowledgements

Neither rain, nor heat, nor knee-deep ice water could keep Mike Worden from joining me on many a journey of exploration. As a police officer, Mike's insights and detective skills were valuable assets, and his sense of humor made hikes—in even the most miserable conditions—fun.

My husband, Bob Strong, has traveled many miles with me through the woods, and through life. May our road ahead be long and full of adventures!

There are so many other people to thank, and I hope I didn't forget anyone: Matthew Thorenz, research librarian extraordinaire at the Moffat Library; Ed Lenik, Martin Brech, Thomas Brannan, and Lou Tartaro, who know so much about stone sites and are kind enough to share their extensive knowledge; Glenn Kreisberg of the Overlook Mountain Center, who is fighting the good fight—and winning—to research and preserve these sites; Shirley Anson of the Plattekill Historical Society, whose enthusiasm for history is contagious; Doc Bayne, who knows the woods like the back of his hand; Erik Gliedman, my favorite photographer, who was willing to go that extra mile—uphill, and with heavy weights; Scott Ditmer and his catalogue of stone chambers; Jim Bonesteel, who is lucky enough to have his very own dolmen; Cathy Taylor of the Upton Historical Commission who is helping to protect a national treasure; Sue Gardner of the Albert Wisner Public Library, who led me to an amazing collection; Bill Pollard, Ferrari specialist and stone chamber researcher; Craig Long, Rockland County Historian; Cliff Patrick, Town of Chester Historian; Elizabeth Werlau, Plattekill Town Historian; Dr. Andrew Smith; Robert Boyle and Kim Stucko of the Field Library; West Milford, N.J. Library; Columbia County Historical Society; and the NYS Department of Environmental Conservation.

About the Author

Linda Zimmermann is a researcher, historian, amateur astronomer, and author of over 30 books. She has made numerous appearances on television and radio. Linda loves the outdoors and enjoys cycling, kayaking, swimming, and hiking, and is intrigued by all things mysterious.

Introduction
by
Michael J. Worden

    Ancient sites have always fascinated me. As a child I used to dream about being an Egyptologist who would find a lost tomb to rival that of King Tutankhamen. I marveled at images of the pyramids of Egypt and Central America, the mysterious Nazca lines, the stone heads of Easter Island, and the intriguing stone circle called Stonehenge. I wanted to be Indiana Jones. I wanted to solve the mysteries of the world. In many ways I still do.

Michael Worden at Stonehenge.

Ancient stone sites seem to be something that exist everywhere else other than here – in the Northeastern United States – and in particular the Hudson Valley region. Ancient cultures all over the world used stone to build tombs, temples and ceremonial structures. They used stone to help them track the movement of the stars and identify important calendar events such as the solstices. They constructed various types of tombs and monuments. Stone is permanent. It doesn't rot like wood. It is a logical choice of material for ancient builders.

I had visited some of the stone chambers in Putnam County with Linda Zimmermann in the past, but my interest in the Hudson Valley stone sites was really piqued during my honeymoon to Ireland in September 2012. As part of the trip, my wife and I visited some megalithic sites, including Carowkeel, the Hill of Tara, Knowth, and the imposing Newgrange. At Knowth and Newgrange, with their impressive passage tombs, I couldn't help but make a startling observation: these passage tombs, in particular their corbeled construction, were very similar in appearance to the Putnam County chambers I had seen. Here I was, in Ireland, far from the Hudson Valley, and I was finding myself having an "ah ha" moment!

The remarkable entrance of Newgrange.

As my wife and I left Newgrange, I had to call Linda and tell her about my experiences. First off, I had to brag that I had been to Newgrange (she had not!), and second to tell her about the observations I had made and how I needed to know more. The Hudson Valley and Northeast stone chambers have been the subject of controversy – with theories that the Celts, Vikings, and other ancient peoples crossed the oceans to make them, to the chambers being nothing more than colonial root cellars, ice houses and sheep pens!

After looking at the ancient Irish sites, maybe the ancient Irish had come to North America and built passage tombs in a manner similar to that back in their native homeland? Perhaps these chambers were evidence of pre-Columbian visitors to the Hudson Valley? Maybe there was a forgotten civilization that once inhabited the region, with their evidence practically hidden in plain sight. It was something worth exploring.

Linda has amassed a wealth of information about this topic. It is truly amazing. Her work with identifying solar and celestial alignments is mind-blowing to me. I wish I could have been more involved in helping her, but demands of my job and family life made that difficult. Yet, I am honored that I had a part in her mission to delve into these sites and their stories. She truly was the Indiana Jones of our many adventures!

What impressed me most, however, was not her open mind, attention to detail, and tenacity. It was her desire to see these sites preserved and studied. More often than I care to recount, I had seen the look of disappointment when she learned that a potential ancient site had been bulldozed to make way for a housing complex or parking lot. During numerous trips we would discuss how many of these sites had been destroyed – gone forever – lost to history. Preservation and serious study of these sites should have been instituted decades ago. We must learn from these past mistakes and begin the serious study and preservation of sites which could help rewrite the history of the Hudson Valley and northeastern United States.

During many of our site visits, we heard stone chambers and structures described as ice houses, sheep pens, root cellars, places to store tanning chemicals, potato storage, and colonial busy work—clever explanations that never seemed to make sense. Now, some of those particular chambers may have been used for these purposes, but that doesn't mean that is why they were built.

I go back to my visit to Newgrange. Our tour guide explained that human ashes had been found inside of Newgrange. Someone in our group asked if Newgrange was a cemetery. Our guide answered, "Just because you find a body doesn't necessarily mean you found a cemetery." Genius. This simple answer fit so well with the many theories about the stone chambers and sites in the Hudson Valley. Yes, they may have been used for many perfectly logical purposes, but I believe the term *repurposing* is more appropriate.

As Europeans settled and discovered these chambers, they simply repurposed them for their own needs. That's just a good use of resources. When life or death depends upon the ability to have adequate shelter, and grow and store food, I see repurposing as a logical explanation. So yes, a farmer may have stored potatoes or even aged his beer in a stone chamber. But that doesn't mean that the farmer built them. Keep that in mind as you evaluate the evidence and information for yourself.

I could go on about the locations of these sites, on hillsides, mountain tops, in the most inconvenient of settings. Then there are the solar and lunar alignments. Were farmers really particular in making sure that their root cellars were properly aligned for the spring equinox? Or the winter solstice? Would farmers be concerned enough to drag large boulders and prop them up precariously? Would they drag large rocks and align them with various celestial events for no apparent reason? Too much thought and planning went into these sites to be coincidental alignments. There was a purpose behind them. They were built for a reason and they were built to last.

Our most recent site visit was to the Upton Chamber in Massachusetts. By far, this was the most incredible chamber I had visited. The long, narrow entry passage and large, corbeled interior construction was very reminiscent of the passage tombs of Ireland. I remember standing in that inner chamber, cold, wet (I had managed to plunge my feet into the frigid, winter water which fills the inner chamber), and physically numb. Despite the less than optimal conditions, it was a moment of inspiration. Using scientific dating methods, this site has been determined to be between 650 and 880 years old. The construction is the same as that seen in the Hudson Valley chambers. It was for me an indication that these chambers – scattered throughout New England and the Hudson Valley—share a similar construction and were perhaps made by people who predate Columbus.

In Avebury, United Kingdom, a Neolithic henge of three stone circles is the largest in Europe and dwarfs nearby Stonehenge. It was there I observed giant stones carefully placed, some of which had odd holes in them. I had seen these holes before: at sites in the Hudson Valley.

Mike inspecting one of the curious holes in the massive stones at Avebury.

Does that mean these sites in Europe are evidence of Irish explorers to the Hudson Valley? Or of Vikings, or Egyptians? Does the argument need to shift from colonial root cellars to ancient seafaring settlers? It could. However, perhaps, the answer is far less complex. Maybe we only need to look closer to home for the answer: our own Native ancestors.

Native peoples built in stone throughout the world. However, here, particularly in the Northeast, stone work has not been commonly attributed to Native Americans. What if history has it wrong? What if the Native Americans used stone, as Linda has so aptly demonstrated, to commemorate celestial events, track the changing of the seasons, and perhaps, ceremonial reasons? Is that such a leap of logic? Maybe our ancestors deserve more credit than they have been given.

Sites scattered throughout the world date back thousands of years and were used for ceremonial purposes, as well as the all-important tracking of the seasons and celestial events important to our ancient ancestors. Pick up any one of the stone sites that Linda has documented here in the Hudson Valley and drop it in Ireland, or Scotland, and no one would question the ancient origin. Not here, though. That site here can't be ancient. It has to have a far more contemporary explanation. At least that is what Linda has been up against in researching this book.

History is constantly being rewritten. The discovery of Göbekli Tepe in Turkey, for example, revealed a complex dating back some 11,000 years. The exact purpose of the complex is unknown, as is who built it. But it was built at a time when humans were not supposed to be building such stone structures. It defied the accepted timeline of history and forced that timeline to be reconsidered.

It's time to do that here, in the Northeast, in the Hudson Valley. Studying these chambers should not be an academic death sentence, but an invitation to expand our collective knowledge and unearth a past which has for too long been forgotten, and is slowly being erased from our future. This is the book which will hopefully begin that transformation.

Stones and Stars

There are mysteries in the woods. There are also mysteries in your backyards, along the roadsides, and in the midst of developments.

There are hundreds of stone sites in New York's Hudson Valley and northern New Jersey that few people have seen, and even fewer appreciate. In fact, there are an estimated 800 such sites throughout New England, and if you were to ask local historians who built them, the vast majority would tell you they were *all* constructed by the early colonists or 18th and 19th century farmers. The prevailing belief is that no one in this part of the country *ever* built anything in stone until the European colonists arrived—even when there is a definitive piece of documentation to the contrary.

On November 30, 1654, John Pynchon wrote a letter to John Winthrop in New Haven, Connecticut about an unusual stone site:

Honored Sir;

Understanding you are now at Newhaven, & supposing there will be opportunity from Hartford for Conveyance thither, I make bold to scribble a few lines to you . . . Sir I heare a report of a stonewall and strong fort in it, made all of Stone, which is newly discovered at or neere Pequet, I should be glad to know the truth of it from your selfe, here being many strange reports about it.
John Pynchon

This site today is known as Gungywamp, and it indeed has many strange stone structures, walls, cairns (man-made piles of rocks), and standing stones. Even with this evidence that at least some of these constructions predated the colonists, the mainstream assertions are still that they are nothing more than colonial root cellars and sheep pens. In addition, one of those alleged root cellars is a stone chamber aligned in such a way that a beam of sunlight enters the rear of the chamber and illuminates a small niche at the front on the days of the spring and fall equinoxes.

Entrance to Gungywamp Equinox Chamber.

Such astronomical alignments are studied in a field known as archaeoastronomy, and it is archaeoastronomy which offers the best evidence to be able to separate the simple root cellars from the ancient calendar sites.

What is the definition of archaeoastronomy? The short answer provided by Professor Robert Hannah, an expert in how ancient cultures perceived and marked time, is that it is "the cultural uses of astronomy." The longer answer is that it is when mankind creates something out of earth, wood, or stone that aligns to some celestial object or event such as a solstice, equinox, star or constellation, or eclipse.

Did colonial farmers really need to spend years studying and recording the positions of the sun, and then exert considerable time and effort hauling and lifting often massive stones to construct root cellars which were also able to tell what time of year it was? Surely, these colonists had the ability to count days, especially when many of them went to church every Sunday, where it was certainly very important to know the date of religious holidays and observances. And, of course, the calendars and almanacs in use at the time allowed them to know the important planting and harvesting seasons.

Winter solstice sunset at Stonehenge in the mid-1980s.
Wikimedia Commons

The most famous, and one of the more elaborate, sites in the world that beautifully illustrates archaeoastronomy is Stonehenge–that magnificent, iconic structure on the plains of Salisbury in England that has numerous solar and lunar alignments, which was constructed over a period from 3000BC to 2000BC. The incredible effort that went into the transporting, aligning, and raising of these enormous stones was remarkable, so obviously being able to know when a date such as winter solstice was occurring was of immense importance to the people of the time.

This is a critical point when examining any site—what was of importance to the builders? We are so used to practically every minute of the day, and every day of the year, being timed and regulated: Catching the 7:15am commuter train, lunch at noon, picking the kids up from soccer practice at 6:00pm, watching your favorite shows from 9:00pm to 11:00pm, and then getting into bed and setting your alarm clock for 6:00am and doing it all over again and again. And if you work in an office or factory, it doesn't really matter if it's January, July, or October, as your schedule is the same.

Commercials starting months in advance let us know how many shopping days until Christmas, when to buy a new grill for your 4th of July barbecue, and when to get gifts and food for all the many other holidays in the calendar. But what if we had no watches, smartphones, Internet, television, or even those cute puppy calendars on our walls? What if the only way we knew what time or month it was, was by watching the sky?

It was something every culture around the world used to do, but modern mankind has lost their connection to the sky. We work all day, watch television or play video games at night, and the movements of the sun, Moon, stars, and planets are of no concern or interest to the average person. Due to light pollution from countless buildings and streetlights in urban and heavily populated areas, many people can no longer see the stars even if they wanted to.

So these modern eyes of ours, these eyes that haven't seen the movements, rhythms, and patterns in the sky, can't be the same eyes with which we look upon ancient sites. We must rip away our techno-centric view of the world and look at things that were important to our ancestors in terms of both religion and survival.

From a sheer survival standpoint, there is a great advantage to knowing when it is time to plant or harvest crops, and gather food and firewood to prepare for the long winter ahead. Early hunters would also have benefited from knowing when certain animals and birds would be migrating.

From the perspective of religion, ceremony, and ritual burials, things aren't so clear-cut, as we can't ever know for certain what was in the hearts and minds of our ancestors. However, we can infer several things from sites from around the world as to what was of importance, i.e., what would make them spend so much time and effort moving and aligning huge stones.

- **Sun**: Marking the solstice (first days of summer and winter) and equinox (first days of spring and fall) sunrises and sunsets, as well as the cross-quarter days (half way between the solstice and equinox). Solar eclipses were also of extreme importance.

- **Moon**: The monthly cycle of the phases of the Moon, eclipses, and the 18.6 year maximum and minimum "lunar standstill."[1]

- **Stars**: Constellations which were seen as figures of people or animals (which, of course, vary from culture to culture) and their interactions with the planets, as well as the brighter and more prominent stars.

- **Transient events**: Comets and supernovae.

- **Cardinal points**: As the sun rose in the east every morning, it was equated with birth, rebirth, and new beginnings. Conversely, as the sun set in the west, that direction was related to death and things ending. (These concepts, for example, have led to both the Pagan and Christian practice of burying people in an east-west direction.) On a purely

---

[1] Just as the sun rises and sets in different positions on the horizon over the course of a year, the moon rises and sets in different positions over the period of 18.6 years.

practical note, knowing where the cardinal points were helped travelers to both navigate on land and sea.

In terms of the archaeoastronomy of any site, then, we need to examine the chance of alignments to any and all of these possibilities. The best way to accomplish this is to make accurate surveys of every site, taking measurements, GPS coordinates, and compass readings. Everything should be photographed on the site, as well as in the immediate surrounding area, and along the horizon, where possible. Best of all, is to personally observe sunrises, sunsets, and the movements of the stars on site.

Over the years, individuals and small groups throughout the Northeast have measured and cataloged many stone sites in the Hudson Valley, but their efforts have not been disseminated to the point where the general public has become aware of them. This information has also not made significant inroads into the academic community, who overall, still relegates all of the sites in to the realm of "colonial farms."

Herein lies one of the many dilemmas of the stone sites. Why is it so earth-shattering, so heretical, to believe that earlier cultures in the Hudson Valley and throughout New England needed to construct calendar sites so that they, and future generations, could tell time?

Everybody Did It

Europe, Asia, Africa, Australia, South America, and North America—all have ancient sites with celestial alignments acknowledged by archaeologists and astronomers. As was previously mentioned, Stonehenge is the most famous, but there are also stone and wood circles, temples, standing stones, chambers, petroglyphs, and cairns around the world in dozens of other countries where people marked time and the passing of the seasons, stretching far back into prehistoric eras.

In the United States, there are astronomical alignments found in the great earthen mounds and "Woodhenge" of Cahokia in Illinois, the Serpent Mound and Newark earthworks in Ohio, Chaco Canyon in New Mexico, the Medicine Wheel in Wyoming, and the Miami Circle in Florida.

6

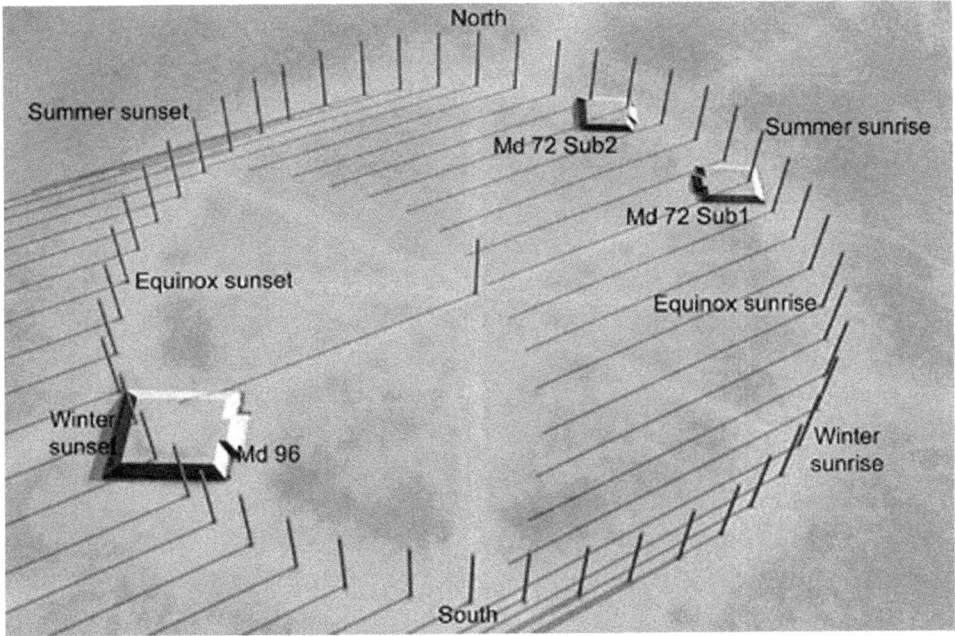

Woodhenge of Cahokia, by Herb Roe.

The facts are clear with the construction of these calendar sites—everybody did it, across the globe, and for thousands of years. So why, then, when it comes to the Hudson Valley, and indeed, the entire Northeast, doesn't mainstream academia consider that there are *any* Native American or pre-Columbian sites where archaeoastronomy can be demonstrated? Why aren't astronomers and archaeologists conducting field studies here? Why should the Northeast be the exception to the global archaeoastronomy rule?

For starters, much of this dismissal of these sites in the Northeast is a reaction to numerous assertions that the stone chambers are energy vortexes, interdimensional doorways, or time-traveling portals. And images of New Age people conducting ceremonies at these sites further alienates professional archaeologists.

Then there was the work of Dr. Barry Fell, who brought many of these sites to public attention in the 1970s with books such as *America, B.C.*, in which he states that several ancient cultures traveled to North America and left their mark. Many of his claims were too much for

7

archaeologists to swallow, and a backlash ensued, prompting such "anti-Fell" publications as the 1980 *Vermont's Stone Chambers*, by Dr. Giovanna Neudorfer, in which she concludes that *every* chamber was a farmer's root cellar.

Popular theories continue to proliferate as to the origins of these sites, although most continue to ignore the real possibility of Native Americans building them. The list is extensive—ancient Egyptians, Phoenicians, Vikings, and Celts being among some of the many foreign cultures thought to have traversed the Atlantic Ocean over the millennia and left their calling cards in stone. While it is certainly possible that any or all of these peoples were able to cross the Atlantic to North America, archaeologists need artifacts and evidence.

The battle rages on even today, with one archaeologist admitting "it would be professional suicide" to study the stone chambers and other sites, due to the wild claims and theories swirling around them. Unfortunately, in such a hostile and negative atmosphere, the real losers are the sites themselves, many of which have been bulldozed to make way for convenience stores and housing projects.

What is needed is a sane, rational, middle ground where the stone chambers, walls, and standing stones speak for themselves by being studied, collecting evidence, and then drawing conclusions based only on the facts. Neither the wild theorists nor the close-minded archaeologists should have a place in this pursuit. Professionals and dedicated amateurs are needed for the sake of science, history, and our heritage—wherever those roads may lead us.

I will try to stick to the middle of those roads—as slippery as they may become. Obviously, for the purposes of this book, I will be focusing on the unusual sites that are not clearly of colonial origins—sites that raise questions that must be answered honestly. My main objectives are to bring awareness of these sites to the general public, and encourage archaeologists, astronomers, and historians to conduct extensive site surveys. If these two things happen, then my ultimate goal may be achieved—the preservation of some of the Hudson Valley's most intriguing—and mysterious—features.

3,000-Year-Old Walls Under the Hudson River?

There is a persistent and pervasive belief in academia that *no one* was building in stone in the northeastern United States until *after* the arrival of the Europeans. With that idea firmly entrenched, all stone structures are relegated to the colonial scrapheap of inconsequential root cellars, animal pens, and boundary walls. But what if just one example could be produced—an example not just a few hundred years before the colonists, but *a few thousand?*

On April 24, 2000, an article entitled *Team Uncovers Hudson's Hidden Features,* written by Wayne A. Hall, appeared in *The Times Herald-Record.* The article described an 18-month-long, $600,000, sonar mapping project of the Hudson River led by Dr. Robin Bell, a marine geophysicist, from Columbia University's Lamont-Doherty Earth Observatory. Among the finds along the river bottom were shipwrecks, reefs, and dead oyster beds. There was also a brief mention of the following:

- Two parallel stone walls, about 20 feet down and 200 feet long, off Storm King Mountain. They are a historic puzzle.

Storm King Mountain
Photo by PointsofNoReturn

Two years later, *Hudson Shipwrecks Found, but No Loose Lips*, written by Kirk Johnson, appeared in the *New York Times*, published December 18, 2002, describing the results of the study in greater detail.

The sonar maps are the unexpected byproduct of a state-financed project to map the river's bottom for habitat and pollution-abatement studies, and because of the thoroughness of the research mandate -- every square foot of river deeper than six feet was scanned -- scientists feel confident that they missed almost nothing.

The article explained that over 200 shipwrecks were found, from Manhattan to Troy, which represented 400 years of history, from important historic ships of the Revolutionary War, to ordinary commercial barges. In order to protect these shipwreck sites from looters and treasure hunters, the actual locations have been kept secret, but general descriptions of what was found were announced, including more information on walls.

The surveys have also turned up more mysterious structures, including a series of submerged walls more than 900 feet long that scientists say are clearly of human construction. They say the walls are probably 3,000 years old because that was the last time the river's water levels were low enough to have allowed construction on dry land.

Walls which are at least 3,000 years old! How was this not a major headline? Who was building walls that long ago in the Hudson Valley? What *other* ancient historic sites are under the river? And, as the two articles are describing sets of walls with vastly different dimensions—200 feet and 900 feet—are there two separate sets of walls in different locations?

I tried contacting Dr. Bell, but she never responded. I then contacted three other project scientists and was told by all three that they remembered the discovery of the stone walls and the interest and excitement they generated. Two said they didn't think they were allowed to reveal their location, but the third wrote the following:

I do remember that we identified some walls in the survey. If I remember correctly they are somewhere in Newburgh Bay (I am not sure I

10

*can reveal the exact locations). They are approx. North-South oriented
and maybe 100m long (not sure about the length exactly). We don't know
what they are made of. Some people thought they might have been some
Indian fishing assembly, but I don't think there is actually an age estimate.*

*The resolution was not good enough to provide more details about
thickness etc. It could be something from 0.5m to a few meters thick.*

To my knowledge they haven't been investigated further so far.

After getting confirmation that these walls do exist from three
separate sources who worked on the project, I then contacted the New
York State Department of Environmental Conservation and requested
more information about these walls. Even though I made it clear that I had
no interest in the shipwrecks, I kind of felt as if I was being viewed as a
potential criminal, wanting to loot these sites. There also appeared to be a
reluctance to officially admit to the existence of these walls, as is shown
by one of the email messages I received:

*There may be a problem in responding to your request in that the
catalog of ship wreck locations and the underlying data that reveals the
wrecks has been deemed exempt from Freedom of Information Law in
order to protect potentially valuable historic artifacts from looting. I think
the "stone walls" that have caught your attention are not obviously stone
walls; they could be the hull of a sunken ship. I will have to clear your
request with NYSDEC's historic preservation officer.*

*In the meantime, just to be sure we are both discussing the same
thing, can you tell me where you heard about these "stone walls"?*

I responded by sending the *New York Times* article and also added:

*I've corresponded with a couple of people associated with the project
who also had the understanding that these were man-made stone walls.
Hopefully, there is a way that information on these features and their
general location can be shared without compromising any shipwreck sites.*

Finally, I was very happy to receive the following message, and the
actual project scan images of the walls! However, despite the release of

this information, it is clear the DEC is not comfortable admitting these may be ancient structures:

Attached is what I can release. The attached images show two parallel topographic ridges several hundred meters long and about 40 meters apart. The ridges are about 0.5 meters high. Whether or not they are stone walls is not at all clear. I think Kirk Johnson was repeating an off-the-cuff remark by whoever he was talking to.

I found it rather curious that this DEC employee would characterize this *New York Times* reporter's mention of the walls, in what is a very detailed article, as simply *repeating an off-the-cuff remark by whoever he was talking to*. In truth, as the article stated, Johnson was talking to none other than Dr. Robin Bell, herself, the head of the project, as well "as Warren Riess, a research associate professor of history and marine sciences at the University of Maine," "Mark L. Peckham, a historic preservation coordinator at the New York State Office of Parks, Recreation and Historic Preservation," and "Frances F. Dunwell, a special assistant for the State Department of Environmental Conservation," the very department in which this employee worked! Clearly, there was nothing "off-the-cuff" about the extensive research and information that went into this article!

Despite all the effort and drama involved in obtaining this information, I was thrilled that my persistence finally paid off, though there are still many questions to be answered. For example, are there two sets of walls, and if so, are they "*20 feet down and 200 feet long, off Storm King Mountain,*" and also somewhere near Newburgh Bay and are as long as 900 feet? Or, is there just that one pair of parallel walls at least "*several hundred meters long and about 40 meters apart.*" Also, with such a potentially important historic discovery, why hasn't more research been conducted on these walls?

Of course, the main question is, if there are stone walls as long 900 feet under the Hudson River, which had to have been built over 3,000 years ago, *who built them*?

If it was the Native Americans living in the Hudson Valley at that time, then we have established a precedence for the existence of indigenous stone builders in the Northeast thousands of years before Columbus was even born.

If it could somehow be proven that the walls were not built by Native Americans, then the gates to pre-Columbian visitation by another culture would be flung open.

In either case, these walls must be further examined by professionals, as the implications of their existence could be a critical turning point in our understanding of the history of the Hudson Valley, the northeastern United States, and possibly other countries across the Atlantic.

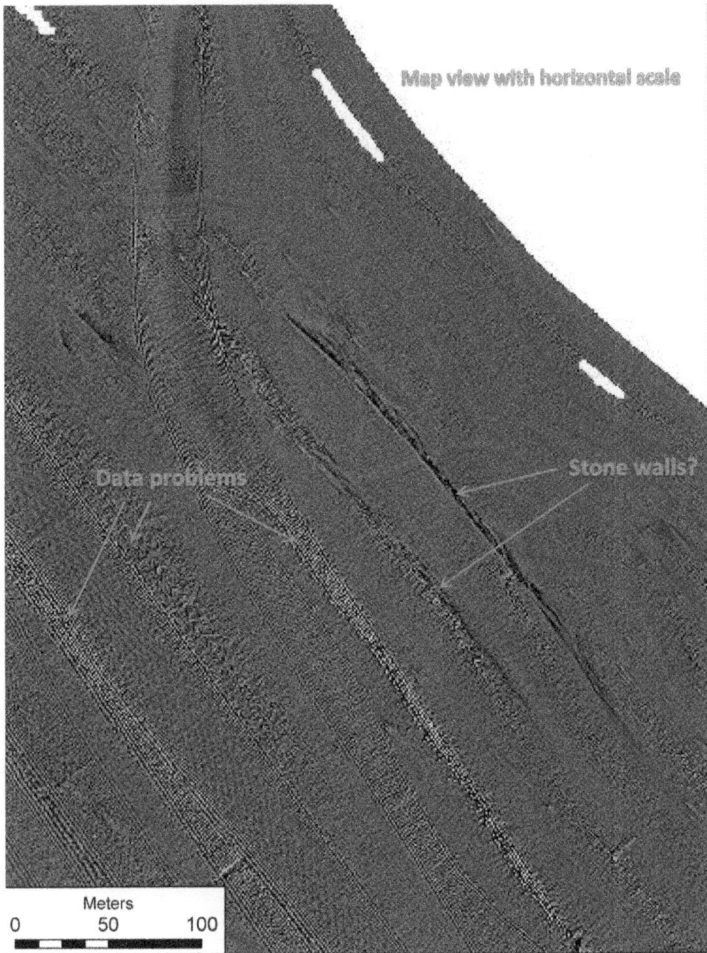

Close up image of the long pair of walls under
the Hudson River released by the DEC.

Map view

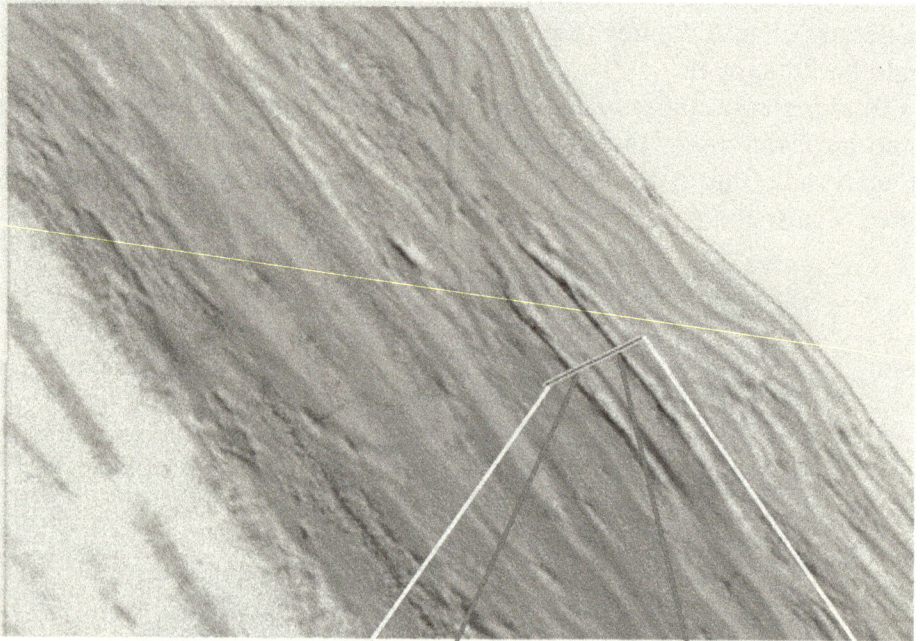

Vertical Profile

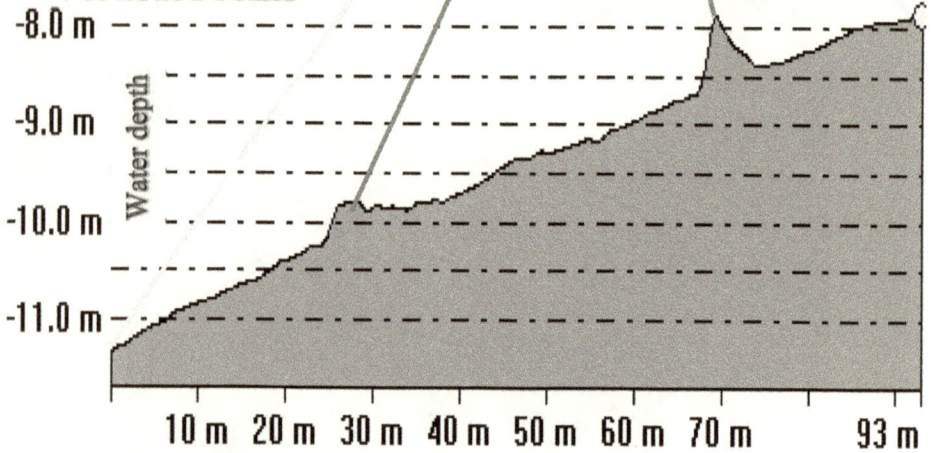

Second image of walls from the DEC.

14

Dolmens and Perched Boulders

Dolmens, cromlechs, and quoits—not exactly household words—but they are all terms to describe something that ancient cultures have been doing for at least 7,000 years: putting large capstones on top of smaller support stones. We can't be certain why all these megalithic structures were built, but some are believed to have been "passage tombs," where the remains of someone of importance or high status were placed. Today, we only see the bare rocks of these structures, but they were most likely originally mounded over with dirt, which has eroded away over the millennia.

While these dolmens are most often associated with the Celts, they are found around the world in Africa, Russia, the Middle East, and India, dating from between 4,000 BC to 3,000 BC. Surprisingly, over 35,000 dolmens have been found in Korea, which accounts for about 40% of the world's total. There, they are known there as *goindal*, or "supported stones." France also has an impressive collection, with at least 10,000 dolmens. However, the country which can boast having the largest such structure of its kind is Ireland and it is known as the Brownshill Dolmen in County Carlow. Its massive capstone weighs in at about 100 tons, or a whopping 200,000 pounds!

The Brownshill Dolmen, photo courtesy of Mike Eldred.

The characteristics of dolmens vary from flat, table-like capstones, to more rounded boulders. However, whether flat or oval, the majority of them are usually positioned so that one end is slanted upwards. The support stones also range from flat-sided, tall pillars, to shorter, rounded or conical stones. The height of the support stones for a dolmen usually allows for someone to walk or crawl underneath the capstone, and would certainly provide enough space for a burial.

Perched boulders, on the other hand, are not usually associated with burials, although they are also large rocks that have support stones. However, those supports are usually much smaller stones than those found in dolmens. Rather than being purpose-built like a dolmen, they appear to be more sites of opportunity, and by that I mean they seem to have been large rocks that were found on or near the site where they now stand, and had been simply propped up and oriented to suit their creators' purposes.

Of course, using the word "simply" may be deceiving here, as there is nothing simple about raising a boulder weighing many tons, turning it in a specific direction, and then placing support stones underneath that are strong enough to obtain the desired height and angle. Finally, perched boulders may stand alone in the landscape, or they may be found in clusters that could be calendar sites.

The 10-foot-long "Tripod Rock" perched boulder in Sussex, NJ.

16

So, if either dolmens or perched boulders were found in the Hudson Valley, or anywhere in the Northeast, wouldn't they upset the archaeological applecart? Wouldn't they be convincing evidence that *someone* was working in stone here for ceremonial or astronomical purposes, possibly thousands of years ago?

In fact, there do appear to be dolmens in the Hudson Valley and New England, and numerous perched boulders. The following are just some examples.

The Glaciers Didn't Do It

In the town of North-Salem, and state of New-York, there is a rock, which from the singularity of its position has long attracted the notice of those who live in its neighborhood, and from its vicinity to the public road, seldom escapes the observation of the passing traveler. It has not, however, it is believed, ever been described. It is situated two miles East of the academy in North-Salem, within thirty feet of the main road to Danbury in Connecticut, upon the sloping brow of a small hill or bank, whose height may be thirty feet. Although weighing many tons, its length being fifteen feet, breadth ten feet, and greatest circumference forty feet; it stands elevated in different parts of it from two to five feet above the earth, resting its whole weight upon the apices of seven small conical pillars; six of these with their bases either united or contiguous, spring up like an irregular group of teeth, and constitute the support of one end of the rock. The remaining pillar, much the largest of them all, stands at the lowest point of that part of the surface over which the rock is elevated, and supports its other end. Notwithstanding the form of the rock is very irregular, and its surface considerably uneven, its whole weight is so nicely adjusted upon these seven small points, one of which is six feet from the others, that no external force yet applied has been sufficient to give it even a tremulous motion.

But the singularity of its position is not the most interesting circumstance which meets the eye of the geological observer. Upon examination, he finds the rock and its pillars composed of entirely different substances. The rock is granite; the pillars which support it are limestone.　　　　　*Rev. Elias Cornelius Salem, Mass. April, 1820*

American Journal of Science, Volume Two, 1820

This is the first known detailed description of what today is called Balanced Rock in North Salem, New York, although it had been recorded by geologists at least as early as 1790. It is indeed a marvel—the massive pink granite capstone weighing an estimated 90 tons, balanced perfectly on its conical limestone supports. While Rev. Cornelius saw this site as a geological natural wonder, a few years later, a British professor of geology and mineralogy, John Finch, saw it as something much more in his article entitled *On the Celtic Antiquities of America*, published in the *American Journal of Science*, Volume 7, 1824.

1824 sketch of Balanced Rock

Finch believed that the history of early America was not as barren and uninteresting as its citizens thought, and stated that this misconception could be changed by:

...calling attention to the rude stone monuments with which their country abounds, although they have hitherto escaped their notice, or been passed over as unworthy of regard.

18

He continued:

On my arrival in this country, I thought I had left the land of Celts and Druids far behind me, and great was my astonishment, on a perusal of Silliman's Philosophical Journal, when I read in the second volume, page 200, to which the reader is requested to refer, the description of a most noble cromlech, although the writer, the Rev. Elias Cornelius, is evidently not aware of the valuable relic of antiquity which he had described... It is a magnificent cromlech, and the most ancient and venerable monument which America possesses, and establishes a common origin between the Aborigines who erected this monument, and the nations who erected similar cromlechs in other parts of the world.

Finch quotes Cornelius' description, which is included above, and then states:

The Geologists in Europe have made an attack upon some of these ancient monuments, and assert that they were produced by the decomposition of rocks of granite; but in this instance the pillars underneath being of limestone, and a large stone on top of granite, and we cannot consider it as the production of nature, because those rocks seldom or never occur in that relative situation. It may also be supposed that it is a boulder of granite, deposited by diluvian torrents in its present situation; but against this opinion, it may be asserted with some confidence, that primitive limestone never appears above the surface of the ground in the shape of small conical pillars, but in large massy blocks, which may be readily seen at some distance.

As a professor of geology and mineralogy, Finch made an excellent observation as to the conical shape of the limestone supports, which to him, clearly indicated they were not natural, but were indeed, man-made. The "diluvian torrents" to which he refers, were massive floods scientists conceived in attempts to explain how huge boulders were found far from where they originated, sometimes on tops of mountains or in the most unlikely locations.

Of course, this was a time when the concept of the Ice Age had not yet taken root in the scientific community. It wasn't until 1840 when Louis Agassiz published his book, *Study on Glaciers*, that the knowledge we now take for granted began to be widely disseminated. These glaciers, sometimes miles thick, carried with them enormous amounts of soil and rocks. As temperatures warmed and the glaciers melted and retreated, they left behind that soil and those rocks, some of which were massive boulders which are called glacial erratics. It is these erratics that were subsequently used to construct some of the dolmens and perched boulder sites in North America.

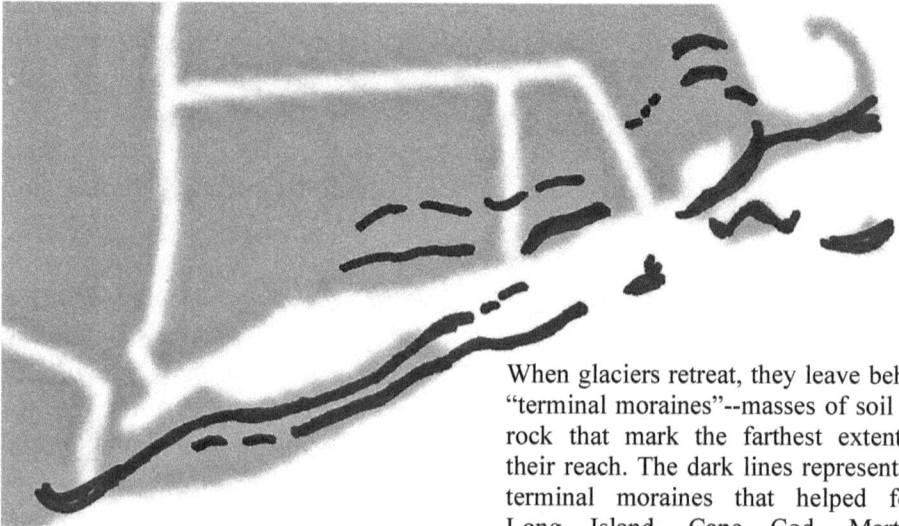

When glaciers retreat, they leave behind "terminal moraines"--masses of soil and rock that mark the farthest extent of their reach. The dark lines represent the terminal moraines that helped form Long Island, Cape Cod, Martha's Vineyard, Nantucket, and Block Island.

So, here we have a British geologist familiar with Celtic stone sites in his homeland, traveling in America, who as early as 1824 saw Balanced Rock as a construction of man. Whether those men were Native Americans, Celts, or someone else, remains to be seen, but the important thing is that 90-ton granite boulders do not position themselves on carved and shaped limestone supports. Or do they?

For many years, scholars and historians believed that Balanced Rock was just a freak of nature—an erratic which just happened to be perfectly placed on top of the seven limestone supports. This should make anyone with any knowledge of geology think twice, as limestone is measured at about a 3 on the Mohs Hardness Scale, where talc is 1, and diamond 10. And according the U.S. General Services Administration article,

Limestone: Characteristics, Uses And Problems, "It is a soft rock and is easily scratched."

How, then, are we to believe that miles of ice in a glacier, crushing the surface of the earth with its tremendous weight, didn't grind these limestone supports into dust, but instead, gently sculpted them all into conical supports, and then softly lowered a 90-ton boulder onto them with perfect balance? Absurd, but this is just what the Historical Society of Salem would have had us believe, as for many years their sign by Balanced Rock stated that it was just a plain, old erratic dropped by a glacier. Only in more recent times, have they finally conceded it may have had man-made origins.

Also, researcher Sal Trento reported that there were circular impressions and discolorations in fields nearby the Balanced Rock, as seen and photographed from an airplane in the 1980s, which may indicate that there were other stone formations, buildings, or ditches and banks like those that are common in Neolithic and Iron Age sites in England. Today, we have the benefit of Google Earth to study the surrounding area, and indeed, there do appear to be circular features, but whether they are ancient structures or the results of more modern farms, can only be decided by conducting an archaeological study. If these circles do have ancient origins, it could establish this area as a complex of significant sites, and help to date the age of the dolmen. Also, a woman who owns a nearby horse farm contacted me to say that she has a stone chamber on her property that is aligned to winter solstice sunrise, adding more weight to the idea that this area was of significant ceremonial and astronomical importance.

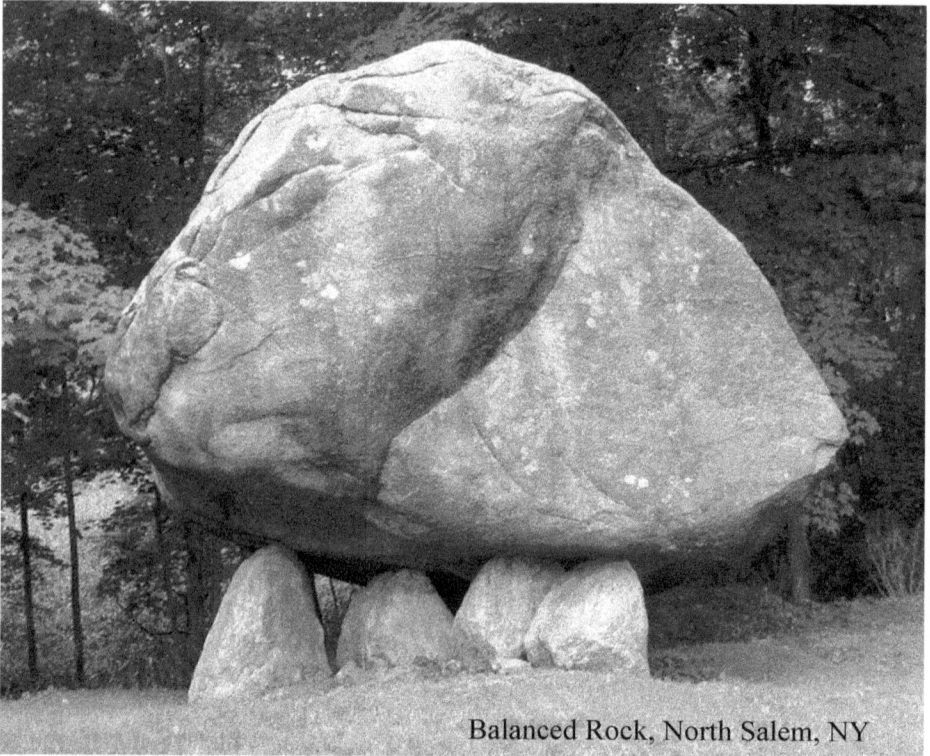

Balanced Rock, North Salem, NY

In a discussion as to whether or not dolmens exist in the Hudson Valley and the Northeast, and are they man-made and of historical significance, providing one clear example should be sufficient to prove a point. Providing another example should then change the nature of that discussion to how these important sites should be studied and preserved.

In Stephentown, New York, about 90 miles almost directly north of the North Salem dolmen, there is another large boulder of similar shape resting on conical support stones. In the 1970s, this stone was reported to have "incised markings," but there were not any further indications as to whether or not this was some form of writing or petroglyphs. Though not of the same massive size, this Stephentown dolmen is very much like its bigger sister in North Salem in shape and positioning.

As this dolmen resides on private property, it is fortunate that the owner, Jim Bonesteel, has safeguarded the structure and chosen not to bulldoze it off his property as others have done at numerous sites over the years. Mr. Bonesteel was also kind enough to take photos of the dolmen, shown below.

Based upon other photos taken in the 1970s when the support stones were more visible, the following sketch illustrates the size and shape of the conical support stones, which look similar to those of the North Salem dolmen.

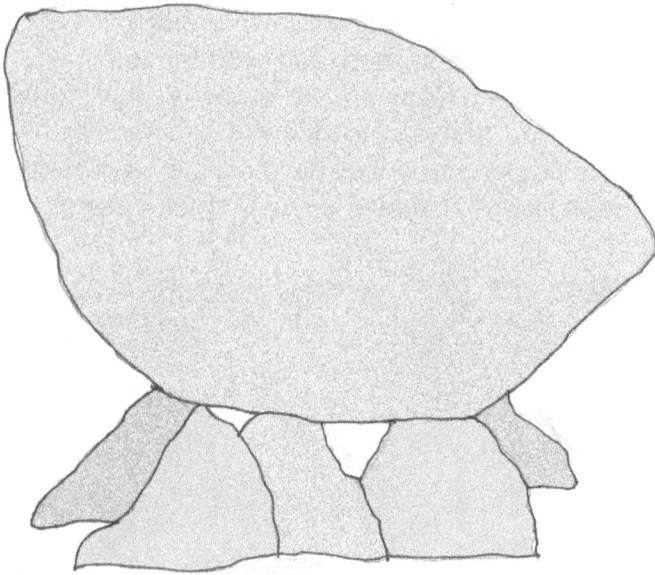

The North Salem and Stephentown dolmens should provide conclusive proof that long ago people in the Hudson Valley were building in stone for purposes we can only relegate under the blanket term of ceremonial. However, as tempting as it is to claim that they are of Celtic origin, a survey of such stone structures shows that people around the globe made dolmens and cromlechs. Without further study, unfortunately, it also cannot be stated that these sites are thousands of years old, although comparatively speaking that is when mankind felt compelled to create these sites in other parts of the world.

What can be stated with some certainty is that there was an enormous amount of effort, planning, and cooperation that had to go into their construction, so obviously they were of great importance to the builders. They should also be of great importance to historians, archaeologists, and geologists, who could shed light on these mysterious structures. In addition to careful examination of the dolmens themselves, the area surrounding these sites should be examined for other archaeological features.

To reiterate the words of John Finch in 1824 in regards to the North Salem site, "It is a magnificent cromlech, and the most ancient and venerable monument which America possesses." Of course, we now know that America also possesses the Stephentown site, as well as several others in New England. And let's hope that future generations come to appreciate them.

Note: Perched boulders will be discussed in more detail in the Calendar Sites chapter.

Balanced Rock is located near 692 Titicus Road (which is also Route 116/121) in North Salem, NY.

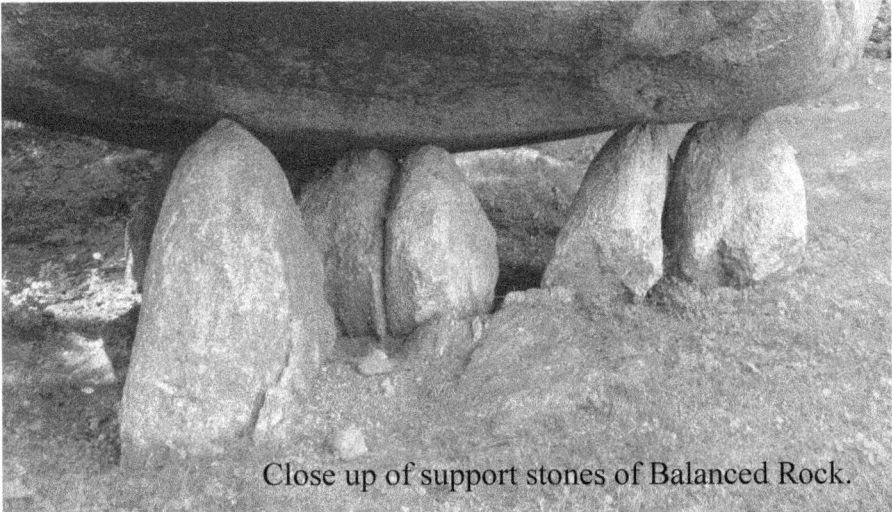

Close up of support stones of Balanced Rock.

The author standing by Balanced Rock to demonstrate how enormous the boulder is, and what an undertaking it must have been to raise and position it.

Stone Chambers

Whangtown Road, Carmel, NY
Winter Solstice Chamber

When I first conceived of this book, I thought the vast majority of the content would involve the stone chambers. Indeed, it was these chambers that initiated my interest in stone sites in the Hudson Valley, and opened my eyes to the possibilities of ancient construction and astronomical alignments. The folder on my computer in which I began saving the hundreds of photos and files for this book was even titled "Stone Chambers."

After years of research, however, the reality set in that the chambers are just one piece of the megalithic puzzle. This doesn't diminish their importance, though. In fact, it enhances their possible significance, as these chambers are not just isolated examples in an otherwise barren landscape. They must be viewed in the context of stone wall complexes, perched boulders, and standing stones, especially when there are astronomical alignments involved—different forms of construction, but all with similar purposes.

Arguably, though, the stone chambers are at the top of the food chain of stones sites, considering the planning and labor that must be involved in building something with such precise alignments. One would hate to carefully raise the corbelled walls, drag several massive roof slabs into place, and then when the sun rose on the desired solstice or equinox, find that the sunlight misses the doorway!

Also, considering how many of my attempts to view solstice or equinox sunrises or sunsets over the years have been thwarted by clouds, rain, and snow, it must have taken many years of observation to determine the exact location for these chambers and other types of stone sites. If I wanted to recreate such a chamber today, I would first build a wooden version and then adjust it as necessary after confirming the alignments through observation. Only then would the first stone be placed.

In any event, hundreds of these chambers were built with great skill and precision, and an entire book cataloguing and describing each one should be written. For the purposes of this book, however, a few of the more notable examples will be explored.

First, though, a few more thoughts and observations as to why most of these chambers are unlikely to be of colonial origin:

- I grew up in Rockland County on the west side of the Hudson River, and believe me, it was aptly named as there are a lot of rocks. But the county was also blessed with good soil for farming—once the rocks were cleared. The Dutch first began settling there in the 1600s, with the English soon following, and then people of many nationalities. Yet for all the farms and all the rocks in Rockland County, there is not a single stone chamber like those in Putnam County—not one. There aren't any in neighboring Orange County, either, which is also on the west side of the river and had many farms. If these stone chambers were built by farmers as root cellars, why was the practice limited to the east side of the river, predominantly in Putnam County?

- A root cellar needs a door, yet most of the chambers show no signs of ever having had any type of door. Some farmers clearly repurposed chambers on their property by adding wooden doors, but these are obviously post-construction additions.

- Some repurposed chambers have concrete in their interiors, but these are crude attempts to add concrete in between the stones post-construction. If a farmer had originally built the chamber, why wouldn't he have used concrete during its construction? Why use the dry stone, mortarless technique of building a chamber, and then try to add concrete later? Most of the concrete in these chambers has not lasted well and is crumbling, while the original stone walls are still standing firm.

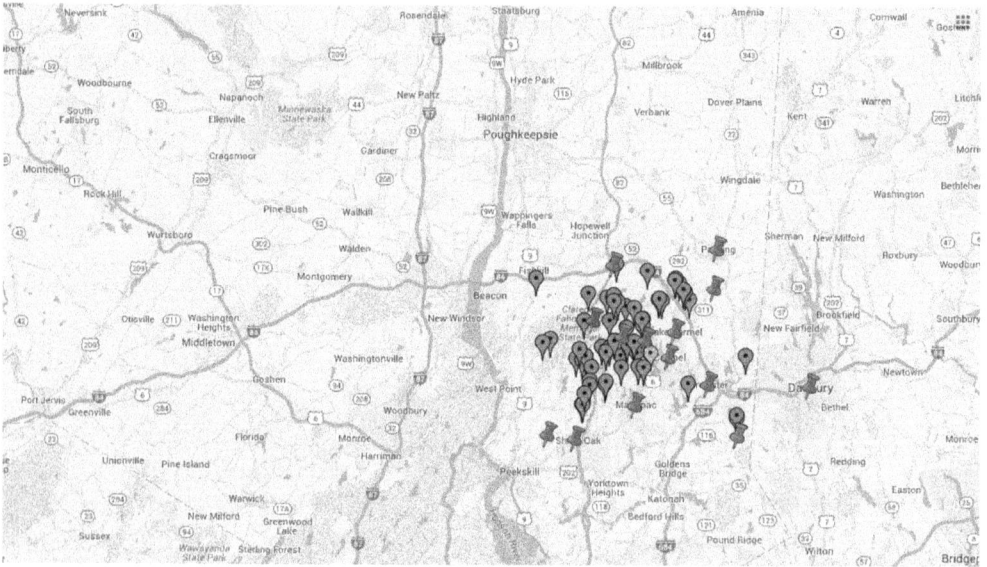

If a picture is worth a thousand words, then the Delong-Cooke map[1] speaks volumes regarding the distribution of stone chambers in the Hudson Valley. Hundreds of chambers were built in Putnam County, yet despite thriving farming communities in the surrounding areas, there is not a single one, making it unlikely that these were built as farmer's root cellars.

- The stone chambers don't have any sort of ventilation, and according to www.commonsensehome.com: "**Root cellars must have ventilation!** This is one of most common mistakes that people make when designing/installing them. Proper ventilation moves the ethylene gas that causes spoilage away from the produce, increasing your storage time and the quality of the items in storage. It also slows down molds and mildews

---

[1] The Delong-Cooke Stone Structure Map (available on Google) has mapped many of the stone sites in the country. Though not complete and having some inaccurate information, it is an excellent resource for locating these sites and getting descriptions.

and other fuzzy things that thrive in dark, damp, still environments."

- In William Corliss' book *Ancient Structures*, which is part of his *Catalog of Archaeological Anomalies*, he states: "To our knowledge, early American farmers used almanacs and not stone alignments to plan their work. Astronomical features, therefore, could undermine the colonial theory of chamber origins."
- Corliss was skeptical of "Precolumbian adventurers from Europe" building these chambers, but goes on to say that "Despite these cautionary remarks, there are some stone chambers in the subject area that seem to betray more sophisticated astronomy. Such 'advanced' features <u>do</u> suggest that perhaps these particular chambers were not constructed solely for the winter storage of vegetables."
- Corliss does concede that Native Americans were "well-attuned to the motion of the sun, Moon, and stars...If Native Americans built some of the controversial chambers for ritual purposes, as some suppose, it would be quite understandable if the doorways sometimes framed the sunrise at one of the solstices. This would be elementary astronomy for Native Americans."
- In their book *Manitou*, Mavor and Dix write: "We see stone chambers as but one of many elements of a ritual architecture in New England that is part of a long, profound, and continuing tradition including the natural landscape and many types of indigenous man-made structures. To consider stone chambers in isolation or solely part of a nearby farmstead or other settlements is a distortion of the record. We see antecedents for most chambers in similar stone structures with established provenance among Native Americans in other parts of North America."
- The chamber in Upton, Massachusetts (see the end of this chapter) not only has important astronomical alignments, but scientific dating techniques have been used to establish that it is of pre-colonial construction. *This sets a crucial precedence*: If there is *one* astronomical chamber that is pre-colonial, it

29

proves that some group of people was present in North America with the means and desire to build these chambers.

The Old Mine Road: Oral History Gone Wrong

Giovanna Neudorfer's 1980 book, *Vermont's Stone Chambers*, was clearly written to discredit the rampant spread of Celtic theories of origin put forth by Barry Fell in *America, B.C.* In fact, the book's forward, written by William Fitzhugh of the Smithsonian Institution, plainly begins:

Fifteen years ago these chambers rested peacefully in the Vermont uplands, and most who knew of their existence did not consider them at all unusual. Today, the chambers are notorious, having been touted as the remains of European Neolithic or Bronze Age settlers. Based on vague architectural similarities with megalithic monuments in Western Europe and the occasional presence of markings, thought to be inscriptions written in various early writing systems, these claims have been advanced by individuals who generally lacked professional training in archaeology, history, or linguistics.

So clearly what was needed then was research by a professional archaeologist on the chambers of Vermont, which was where Neudorfer, the Vermont State Archaeologist, came in. She undertook a study and surveyed dozens of chambers, taking careful measurements. She also sifted through documents and conducted interviews to learn the oral history of a location. While I applaud the work she did, throughout the book I was surprised to see how much she ultimately relied on "oral evidence" to bolster her colonial origins argument.

In other words, a letter from an elderly woman who claimed that a certain chamber was built by her great-grandfather to store apple cider, seemed to be as valid as if she had obtained a radiocarbon date. Maybe that chamber was built for apple cider, but the fact that Neudorfer heavily relied on oral evidence to draw her conclusions made me think about the incredible unreliability of such alleged "proof."

For example, how many times have people brought objects to the *Antiques Road Show*, convinced that their ancestor received the item from the hand of Napoleon himself—only to find out that the object was not even made until 50 years after Napoleon had died. In the Hudson Valley, how many homes lay claim to the belief that "George Washington slept here!" Also heard quite often, is that a house was used to help slaves escape on the Underground Railroad. These are all great stories, but family histories are notoriously wrong. Sometimes, even historians are terribly wrong.

Case in point, the famous Old Mine Road, for which plaques were commemorated and books were written. This 104-mile road was supposedly hacked out of the wilderness in the 1650s by Dutch colonists, through hostile Indian territory, all the way from Kingston, NY to the Pahaquarry Copper Mine on the Delaware River in New Jersey. Everyone *knew* these were the facts, because oral history told us so.

NEW YORK

OLD MINE ROAD

OLDEST 100-MILE ROAD IN AMERICA. BUILT BY DUTCH MINERS BEFORE 1664 FROM KINGSTON TO COPPER MINES NEAR DELAWARE WATER GAP

STATE EDUCATION DEPARTMENT 1935

Unfortunately, oral history was wrong. The truth is:

- The "Old Mine Road" actually began as an ancient Indian trail.
- In the 1650s, there simply weren't enough men in Kingston to cut down a hundred miles of huge, old-growth trees and build a road.

31

- There were three wars with the Native Americans during the mid-1600s. Wandering deep into Indian lands to chop down their trees would have been suicide.
- The quality of copper ore at the Pahaquarry Mine is extremely low, just about two percent, and it required special processing capabilities which the Dutch settlers did not possess. It would make no sense to haul heavy, useless ore over a hundred miles through the wilderness.
- Last, and certainly not least, there has never been any archaeological evidence that the Dutch ever mined at Pahaquarry, or built the road.

The case of the Old Mine Road should be used as a cautionary tale about oral evidence. Maybe your sweet, old grandma heard family stories about that stone chamber, perched boulder, or cairn on her property, but what does the radiocarbon dating say about its age? What does the archaeoastronomy say about the alignments at the site? Before any site is dismissed or discounted, let's first get the facts—*all* the facts.

King's Chamber
Putnam Valley, NY

A constant source of frustration and wasted time is the lack of specific directions and locations to actually find these sites. The search for the King's Chamber in Putnam Valley, New York—so called, as it is one of the largest—was just another example. There were photos and vague directions online, but no one said, "Park here, walk this direction, for this distance, to these coordinates."

Based upon one of these nebulous references, my husband, Bob, and I set out several years ago to give it our best shot. What little information was available said to park on Pudding Street and just "head into the woods." Unfortunately, however, there were no trails, and the dense sticker bushes quickly turned the hike into a pain tolerance test. As there also had recently been a prolonged period of heavy rains, much of the landscape was flooded. Wet and bleeding, we finally abandoned the hike. So much for our first attempt.

While planning a new strategy, I just happened to meet someone from that area during an unrelated project. I mentioned the King's Chamber and to my astonishment and delight, she said she had just been there a few days earlier! She told me to park on Porter Street in Putnam Valley, and that there was a trail to follow which leads right to the chamber.

I didn't waste time once I had this information, and Bob and I found the tiny parking area—maybe big enough for two cars—on Porter Street and headed out with great optimism, until we came to a "T" on the trail by a dilapidated garage or storage building. Having no idea whether to turn left or right, I began to despair that this would become another wild goose chase. Just then, we heard a sound, and a lone female jogger appeared on the trail to our left. As she passed by, I asked if she knew the location of the stone chamber.

"That way," she said, pointing behind her and not missing a step.

That day, and on the many subsequent hikes I have taken to this chamber over the years, I have *never* encountered anyone else in those woods. We were very lucky that the jogger was there at that particular moment!

But of course, as is so often the case, the trail we needed to take went up a steep hill. Bob and I constantly scanned the woods around us searching for the King's Chamber, or the smaller chamber that was supposed to be nearby. We passed a 20th century shelter with a stone fireplace used by campers, and there were other signs of more recent times, such as some water pipes. The trail itself had apparently been a colonial road, although we didn't see any foundations or remnants of homes or barns.

Finally, off to our right, we spotted the smaller chamber. Even though I was a bit winded from going uphill, I couldn't help but run over to it. Unfortunately, the large lintel stone at the entrance has fallen, but the remainder of the structure looked safe enough to go inside. Of particular interest, was the long, rectangular stone in the base of the back wall, which could be viewed as a bench, a bed, or an altar, depending upon your interpretation and theoretical leanings. This type of feature has been found in other stone chambers in the Northeast, but it is not common. The purpose of this rectangular stone may be related to the fact that the light of the winter solstice sunrise illuminates this back wall. Did observers sit here to watch the special event?

33

The damaged chamber.

While this was indeed a fascinating chamber, where was the King's Chamber? It wouldn't be long before we would find it, as we got back on the trail and a short distance ahead there was the main objective of our search—its wide doorway looking like a gaping, black hole in the woods. Once again, I found myself running towards it.

One of the first things one notices upon approaching it, is that this chamber is not only of an unusual size, it has a standing stone in front of it. There it is a lot of controversy about this stone, because there are photos of the chamber in recent times in which there is no stone standing. This has led at least one local historian to harshly criticize what she characterized as the Celtic/Druid enthusiasts who erected the stone to fabricate evidence of early European construction. In reality, the stone had simply appeared to have fallen out of its "socket," and was lifted back into place with the best of intentions by NEARA[2] members.

The interior of the damaged chamber with the stone bench at the back.

This standing stone controversy illustrates the need to leave things where you find them, and to document everything with photographs or sketches. Even if this stone had stood in that socket for centuries—which I believe is probable—the fact that someone picked it up and put it back is

---

[2] The New England Antiquities Research Association, NEARA, promotes "disciplined research on the origin and functions of North American lithic structures and related landscape features. Through its publications and meetings, NEARA shall provide an open forum for discussion and debate on the significance of such sites within their cultural context. NEARA shall also engage in advocacy for public awareness of the need to preserve these sites." Please go to their informative website: www.neara.org

enough for some archaeologists and historians to conclude that such tampering invalidates any possible significance.

The entrance to the King's Chamber and the controversial standing stone.
Note: The standing stone was recently knocked down in an apparent act of vandalism.

There is also some question as to the original size of the King's Chamber. In an article written by several NEARA members, *Archaeo-Astronomical Prospecting at the Moose Hill Stone Chambers*[3], the authors suggest that the 33-foot-long chamber was lengthened in the front and a new doorway was added at some point, possibly even as late as the 19th century. Part of their reasoning for this is that certain astronomical alignments would fit better with a shortened chamber.

The interior of the long King's Chamber with its twelve, massive roof slabs.

Whether or not this is true, the team did find that there are several boulders on ridges within view of the "plaza" in front of the King's Chamber which appear to have alignments to the solstices and equinoxes. While being careful to point out that these stone positions are not *definitely* the work of man, they do calculate that the chance of the random

---

[3] *Archaeo-Astronomical Prospecting At the Moose Hill Stone Chambers*, Frederick W. Martin, Elizabeth F. Martin, Polly Midgley, and Walter Wheeler, *Archaeology of Eastern North America*, 2012, Vol. 40, p145-162.

placement of these boulders by a glacier, resulting in solstice and equinox alignments, is less than one percent. And, there may also be alignments with the 18.6 year lunar cycle at this site.

Their paper ends with the following statement:

We conclude that the character of the stone remains which surround the Moose Hill chambers suggests pre-contact construction and that therefore the plaza, some of the skyline stones, and the chambers themselves deserve detailed investigation by subsurface archaeological techniques.

I cannot agree more that dating tests should be performed on both of these chambers, as well as having additional astronomical work conducted. Another possibly important thing I noticed in their map of the site was that there are four rocks that are in the same relative positions to one another as the four Pleiades cairns at the Ramapo Walls (see Calendar Sites chapter). I placed a transparency of the brightest stars of this cluster over an enlargement of the map, and the same four stars that fit over the four cairns, also fit over these rocks *exactly*. If this is a calendar site, it is doubtful that this is just a coincidence. There may also be a Pleiades setting sighting alignment with these four stones and some of the openings in the walls, but that is only speculation based upon the map, and will need to be studied at the site.

Another odd thing here is the profusion of walls. While some may be colonial boundary walls, others start and stop for no discernible reason and don't appear to mark any sort of boundary. Some walls form small rectangles with no entrances, while others continue up and over the tops of high rock outcroppings—fitting neither the context for agriculture or livestock management. And if it was simple field clearing, who would be crazy enough to carry heavy stones *to the top* of a ledge or rock outcropping?

Directions: Park on Porter Street in Putnam Valley, NY, in the small space on the left side of the road. Follow the trail to the dilapidated shed, then turn left and go up the hill. You will come to the smaller, damaged chamber first, on your right. Follow the trail a little further to the King's Chamber, which is at N 41.42060 W 073.78925

Where is the Proof?

"A date this old should have quickly brought academic archaeologists running to the site, but no one in science's mainstream seemed interested!"
William Corliss, *Ancient Structures*

In the ongoing ancient megalithic battle between professional and amateur archaeologists, the professionals inevitably—and rightly so—continue to ask, "Where's the proof?" Theories are not evidence, and science needs evidence. One of the best tools available to gather evidence is radiocarbon dating, which has been in use since its development in the late 1940s. By examining a radioactive isotope of carbon present in living things, scientists have been able to accurately date wood, charcoal, human bones, and other organic material at archaeological sites.

What should be a sure way to end the debate as to whether at least some of the stone chambers predate the colonial era would be to obtain radiocarbon dates. In fact, this was done in 1978 at a stone chamber in Windham County, Vermont, and the result was astonishing – organic material found in the chamber was 1,405 years old, plus or minus 190 years. This means that the chamber was already built and in use somewhere between 420 A.D. and 800 A.D., and could possibly be even much older than that.

Physicist and author William Corliss, who wrote many volumes about anomalies in science, tended to side with the colonial root cellar theory of chambers in America, but even he had to concede that it was puzzling why this evidence didn't receive proper attention. In his book *Ancient Structures*, Corliss commented, "A date this old should have quickly brought academic archaeologists running to the site, but no one in science's mainstream seemed interested!"

In this same book, Corliss also mentions radiocarbon dates obtained at America's Stonehenge complex in New Hampshire, which ranged from 520 A.D. to over 3,500 years old.

Fifteen miles away in Newton, New Hampshire, there is a stone chamber which has a unique solar alignment. Only at winter solstice sunrise does a shaft of light appear at the intersection of the back wall and one of the sidewalls. In addition to a stone scraping tool and some clay potsherds recovered from the site, a piece of charcoal was unearthed from the dirt piled on top of the chamber. It was found 15 inches deep and about 2.5 inches above one of the roofing stones, so it had obviously been produced sometime after the chamber was built. That charcoal dated to about 1100 AD.

If not ending the debate about the age of these particular sites, these dates *should* have brought archaeologists running to these chambers and America's Stonehenge, but yet again, they were all but ignored. Corliss said, "When asked about these dates, the professional archaeologists suggested that the samples had been contaminated." Three different sites, four different radiocarbon dates showing they were built and in use at least a thousand years before the colonial era, yet each result was shot down as "contaminated" samples.

There appears to be a double standard here, and to be fair, it is on both sides of the debate. Evidence that bolsters one side's argument is considered invalid by the other side. And it is not only with radiocarbon dates that this has occurred. Ancient coins, inscriptions, and artifacts that have been found at stone sites or other locations in the Northeast have universally been ascribed to fraud, misinterpretation, or contamination.

Frustration on the part of the ancient theorist is therefore understandable--don't ask "Where's the proof?" and then ignore the evidence.

Whangtown Road Chambers
Carmel, NY

Many years ago I had heard about the Whangtown Road chambers in Carmel, NY, which were supposed to be oriented to the winter solstice and the equinox sunrises, but my curiosity was really piqued when I came upon a photo on the Internet taken in 2008 by former local legislator Lou Tartaro, who has been studying these stone sites for decades. His photo showed the Solstice Chamber blanketed in snow, with the soft light of the winter solstice dawn squarely framed by the doorway and illuminating the back wall of the almost 29-foot-long stone chamber. It was a mesmerizing picture, and I wanted to get to this site as soon as possible.

I contacted Lou during the winter of 2015 and he generously volunteered to take Mike Worden and I to the chambers. Unfortunately, the snow was very deep and the temperatures were very low, and our scheduled hike was rescheduled, and then rescheduled again, until we gave in to Mother Nature and stopped trying. Finally, on the spur-of-the-moment during a return trip from Connecticut in the spring, Bob and I decided to see if we could find the chambers on our own. I had looked at a couple of hiking maps and knew where they were supposed to be—in theory—but I have often found that one man's directions are another's ticket to getting completely lost.

We decided to follow the circular, red, hawk's head trail markers from the parking area at the end of Whangtown Road, as the famous Hawk Rock is supposed to be along the same trail. It's sometimes difficult to gauge distances when hiking—especially when going uphill most of the way—and I didn't know how far off the trail the chamber would be, so we took our time and made sure we didn't pass it by. We were encouraged by the sighting of some large stone walls, but there were no chambers next to them. We split up to cover more ground and I was beginning to feel the despair one gets in the woods when one has no idea where to find something. Then I heard Bob's distinctive whistle to signal that he had found a chamber.

It was a great relief, and we took many photos and thoroughly examined the chamber inside and out. With so many leaves on the trees, the horizon was impossible to see, but by using one of the features on my Garmin GPS unit while I stood facing out of the doorway, I was able to determine that sunrise, directly in front of the chamber, would occur between two hills, which must be a dramatic sight. The Garmin also indicated that the direction was about 120 degrees, which was indeed the direction where the winter solstice sunrise would be. It was all very exciting!

The 3D view on the Garmin Oregon 450t shows that
winter solstice sunrise occurs right between two mountains.

Of course, the mainstream view is that this chamber is "just another colonial root cellar" from the Mead farm that was here for a number of years in the mid-1800s. However, when looking at the pathetic, sparse, few stones that remain of the one-room Mead farm house, it defies all logic that anyone would construct their home in such a shoddy manner that it would crumble to nothing, yet build their root cellar to withstand the ages—not to mention taking the time to precisely align it to the winter solstice sunrise!

Our next task was to try to find the Equinox Chamber which was supposed to be nearby. We scoured the surrounding woods, but couldn't find any trace of it, until I happened to see what looked like the faintest of possible paths through some tall weeds. A few steps later, and there was the Equinox Chamber on the side of a very steep hill. My first thought was that there was no way a farmer was going to be able to pull a wagon full of potatoes in front of this chamber—not to mention wasting time orienting the doorway to the spring and fall equinox sunrises.

The Whangtown Equinox Chamber is on the side of a steep hill
and obscured by vegetation.

Unfortunately, the lintel stone over the doorway of this chamber has an ominous-looking crack, and there has been a partial collapse in the back, so we didn't feel it was safe to go inside. But I was still able to position myself in the doorway and determine that the opening did indeed face out to 90 degrees—right where the sun would rise over the horizon on the first days of spring and fall.

The lintel stone is dangerously cracked, and there is a partial collapse inside. Using a powerful 18 million candlepower light, I was able to simulate the direction of equinox sunrise, which would have illuminated the back of the chamber if not for the partial collapse.

One of the pro-root cellar arguments I have heard, was that facing the doorway in a particular direction—say in this case, due east—was ideal for letting in just the right amount of light. If so, then why are these two chambers, located within sight of one another just 271 feet apart[4], facing

---

[4] This is a tantalizing measurement that has come up at other sites. During Alexander Thom's survey of 600 megalithic sites in Europe, he believed that he found a common unit of measurement used by all the builders, the megalithic yard, which he said was 2.72

43

in different directions? If a certain direction was the recommended way to store your precious root vegetables, why deviate, and on the same property?

Furthermore, why weren't all of the almost 200 chambers in and around Putnam County oriented in the same general direction? They obviously all shared a similar corbelled-wall, slab-roofed, dry stone construction technique, so why wasn't proper orientation part of the learning process? According to several root cellar websites, doorways in the southern states should face north, while it is just the opposite for northern states. To maximize sunlight in the chamber in these colder regions, doorways should be facing 180 degrees, or due south.

Yet, according to one survey of 50 chambers in the area, not a single one faced 180 degrees. In another catalogue of over 75 chambers, just five faced south. The majority of all the others in these two surveys faced one of three directions—toward equinox sunrise, or toward winter solstice sunrise or sunset. In fact, there is a third Whangtown chamber nearby, known as the Mother Earth Chamber, that is also facing winter solstice sunrise. Proper orientation did indeed appear to be a very important aspect in the planning and construction of these chambers, but *not* so that "Joe Colonial" could store his turnips and potatoes. *The position of the sun itself* seems to be the motivating factor.

We made another trip to the two chambers that summer to take more photos and measurements, and take a better look at the surrounding area. There are numerous low walls running in all directions which could simply be from field clearing or boundary markers. However, there are two large stone walls that were completely different. On a subsequent trip (described below), Lou Tartaro said that the shorter of the two walls (measuring 63 feet in length, and over 6 feet high) was most likely part of a barn, but the other longer, more massive, wall (88 feet in length, over 6 feet high, and varying in width from 6 to 16 feet) remains a mystery.

---

feet. That would make 100 megalithic yards equal 272 feet. While some scholars have discounted the megalithic yard, I have found at least five cases at sites in the Hudson Valley where I have made measurements of walls and distances of about 272 feet. I did not set out to look for things in megalithic yards, but as that number came up several times, it is at least worth mentioning. One occurrence is of no consequence, twice could be a coincidence, but five times may indicate a pattern.

The 88-foot-long wall was built with some very large stones, and doesn't appear to have had any discernable purpose.

Of course, measurements and calculations are all well and good, but nothing compares to witnessing an actual solar alignment firsthand! Bad weather was forecast for both December 21 and 22 of 2015, but Sunday the 20th was supposed to be clear, and Bob and I were determined to take advantage of that rare opportunity. As luck would have it, though, my family's Christmas party was the night before, so when the alarm went off at 4:45am Sunday morning after just a few hours of sleep, it was a battle of science over fatigue—but of course science won!

It was about a 45-minute drive from our home to Whangtown Road in Carmel, and the trail was shrouded in darkness when we started to ascend. Thanks to both a headlamp and handheld flashlight, we were able to safely navigate over fallen trees and rocks, and *not* wander off the trail. As the horizon began to slowly lighten, my heart beat a little faster and we picked up the pace. I felt like a kid on Christmas morning rushing to see what presents were under the tree.

As we impatiently waited in the darkness for sunrise, three other people arrived; two men and a woman. The woman asked my name, and when I told her, she knew who I was and pointed to one of the men and said he was Lou Tartaro! You never know who you will meet at a solstice! The other man and the woman were members of NEARA and were also quite familiar with chambers in the area, so it was very good to share the experience with people who appreciate these sites.

Bob stood atop the chamber as our solar lookout, and it wasn't long before we could see that our shadows were being cast on the back wall when we stood in the doorway. Finally, the sun peeked over the horizon, and while it was not quite the actual day of the winter solstice, we were still treated to a spectacular sight, and I will let my photo speak for itself.

After we took all our outside photos, we went inside the chamber to see how it looked from that perspective. Lou pointed out a fascinating feature of the doorway; it is slightly shorter in width on the left side. This is no accident, as it was intentionally designed and built that way to maximize the time the rectangle of winter solstice sunlight illuminates the back wall of the chamber! The amateur astronomer in me was doubly impressed with the planning and careful construction that had to go into this site.

Looking out of the Winter Solstice Chamber minutes before sunrise.

To me, it just doesn't make sense that a simple farmer trying to scratch a living out of this rocky soil would have had the time, skill, and knowledge necessary to haul massive stones into such precise alignments—and for what possible purpose!? And then we are supposed to believe that he did it all again in another chamber to mark the equinoxes as well? All the while living in a poorly-constructed one-room shack?

Once the sun had risen beyond the reach of the chamber doorway, we started to head back along the trail. We came upon another group of people—obviously New Age-types—who were going to the chamber with some odd instrument or shaman stick to conduct a solstice ceremony. I have plenty of my own strange beliefs so I'm not throwing stones, but it is images of dancing Neo-Druids playing flutes and tossing flowers that mainstream scientists point to when trying to discredit any pre-Columbian theories about the construction of these sites. Lou told me that he had even witnessed ceremonies at the Equinox Chamber where participants were happily throwing eggs to welcome the spring!

Odd rituals aside, I invite any archaeologists, astronomers, and historians to stand in the winter solstice sunlight of a chamber such as this and declare it was just a root cellar built by an ordinary farmer, who by accident created this precise alignment.

Directions: In order to visit this site, you must obtain a Department of Environmental Protection permit, which is free. You can register online at: http://www.nyc.gov/html/dep/html/recreation/index.shtml

Park in the small lot at the end of Whangtown Road, Carmel, NY. Get there early on weekends as the lot often fills up by mid-morning. Take the red hawk's head trail (maps are available online). The trail goes uphill, and once you reach the large stone walls on your right, you are getting close.

The larger winter solstice chamber will be on your right. To find the partially collapsed equinox chamber, get back on the trail, and a short distance away on your left, look for a short path down a hill. The chamber is just a few feet from the trail, but can't be seen from it as it is in the side of the hill.

The Mother Earth Chamber, which has an unusual stone entranceway, can be found further down the trail and taking a left fork. By continuing on the red-marker trail, you will eventually come to a huge rock known as Hawk Rock, as it resembles a sitting hawk.

GPS Coordinates:
- Wall 1: N 41.47874, W 073.69714
- Wall 2: 41.47919, 073.69763
- Winter Solstice Chamber: 41.47801, 073.69765
- Equinox Chamber: 41.47766, 073.69724
- Mother Earth Chamber: 41.476377, 073.692243

(Note: Wall and Winter Solstice and Equinox Chamber coordinates were personally obtained using a Garmin Oregon 450t. Mother Earth Chamber coordinates are from the Delong-Cooke map.)

Although this is not a site in the Hudson Valley, I am including this section as it has important lessons to be learned—lessons applicable to stone sites everywhere.

Upton, Massachusetts: A Tale of Two Sites

The tale of the Upton Chamber and Pratt Hill represents everything that is right and wrong in regards to stone sites in the northeast. It is a story of hope and despair, of research and disinterest, and preservation and destruction.

Although the colonists knew of the chamber in the early 1700s, the first written account of it was published in an 1893 issue of the *Milford Journal*, in which the author wonders at the mystery of its origins. It is a mystery the people of Upton still embrace, according to Cathy Taylor, Chairwoman of the Upton Historical Commission. In January of 2016, Cathy was kind enough to give Mike Worden and I a tour of the chamber and nearby Pratt Hill—which was a tale unto itself—but first some background on the sites.

When approaching the Upton Chamber, it looks like a dark hole in the side of an embankment. Only the lintel and facing stones are visible, and they gave no clue as to what lies beyond. Ducking down to enter the approximately five-foot-high doorway, you pass through a narrow, fourteen-foot-long, irregularly-shaped tunnel of sorts.

As your eyes adjust to the sudden darkness, you are unprepared to emerge into an eleven-foot-diameter beehive chamber with a corbeled, ten-foot-high ceiling. And it is all of dry stone construction held together with a capstone at the top, meaning these granite stones are held together without mortar of any kind.

The Upton Chamber was studied by numerous people throughout the 20th century, but the real breakthrough came when James Mavor and Byron Dix led a team of researchers who uncovered some of the chamber's secrets. Their findings are best read in detail in their excellent book, *Manitou*[5], but the following summarizes their amazing discoveries.

On a brief first inspection, they determined that the long entranceway may point toward summer solstice sunset. They also suspected that there may be a boulder or stone mound on the summit of Pratt Hill, about a mile to the northwest, which might form a sighting alignment for the solstice sunset.

In their own words, "This was the moment archaeoastronomers dream of, a chance to check out a theory." However, they were initially dismayed to find that there was not one, but *three* stone mounds on Pratt Hill, each about 45 feet long. Subsequent investigations uncovered many additional mounds of various sizes, as well as walls, and other features. All they had hoped for was one alignment stone, but they quickly realized that the Pratt Hill-Upton Chamber connection went far beyond a single solstice alignment.

After an impressive, in-depth survey of the site and countless calculations, they found that by standing inside the chamber, an observer would not only see the summer solstice sunset over one of the mounds on Pratt Hill, but also the important setting of the Pleiades over two other mounds, along with several other star setting alignments.

They had discovered the *why* of the Pratt Hill–Upton Chamber sites, but there remained the *who* and the *when*. By calculating the dates for the optimum alignments with the stars and mounds, they arrived at a theoretical initial construction period of around 710 AD! While there aren't archaeological artifacts to prove who built the site, obviously, the Native Americans who lived in the area must be given the greatest consideration.

The next major milestone in the research of these sites came in 2011, when the Upton Historical Commission sponsored a project to conduct OSL[6] dating tests. The entranceway was in need of repair, so they took the

---

[5] *Manitou, The Sacred Landscape of New England's Native Civilization*, James Mavor and Byron Dix, Inner Traditions International, Rochester, Vermont, 1989
[6] Optically Stimulated Luminescence dating uses minerals such as quartz and feldspar to determine how long ago they were exposed to sunlight.

opportunity to obtain soil samples from underneath some of the bottom stones. The test results were as follows:

The age of this unit is between 650 and 880 years ago and most probably dates the surface the chamber was built on. These results put the origin of the entranceway to Upton Chamber before documented English settlement of the area. Although there was a European presence on the coastline in Plymouth in 1620 and in Boston in 1630, settlement close by in Mendon did not occur until 1660.[7]

Even considering all the factors for possible errors, the construction date for the entranceway can still be placed between 1350 and 1625, confirming that this was *not* a colonial ice house or storeroom, as some had believed. This was a monumentally important discovery, as here was definitive evidence that stone construction with astronomical alignments was taking place in the Northeast *before* the European colonists. Can mainstream archaeology now begin to consider that other sites may also have pre-colonial origins as well?

The other critically important step taken in regards to the Upton Chamber was that the town purchased the land and created Heritage Park. This has not only preserved the site for future generations to study and admire, but it is now available to the public to experience. I hope the case of the Upton Chamber will be an example to other communities that this is how such sites should be treated–with research and preservation.

Unfortunately, however, the Pratt Hill story did not have such a happy ending.

After reading an article written by Bill Shaner[8] about the OSL testing in which Cathy Taylor is quoted, I contacted her for additional information. She sent me the official reports on the project, and offered to show Mike and I around the sites, with permission granted from the Narragansett Trust. We had scheduled a trip for mid-January, but a heavy rain caused us to postpone it for a week. After all, we wanted to stay warm and dry during our visit...

---

[7] *Construction ages of the Upton Stone Chamber: Preliminary findings and suggestions for future luminescence research*, S.A. Mahan et al. / Quaternary Geochronology, (2015)
[8] *Study Suggests Upton Cave is Native American*, Bill Shaner, *Milford Daily News*, posted on the *Upton Wicked Local News* website, October 24, 2015, http://upton.wickedlocal.com/article/20151024/NEWS/151026998

Mike and I arrived at Heritage Park about half an hour ahead of our scheduled meeting time with Cathy. The location of the chamber eluded us at first, but after scouring the trails, we found it back near the parking area. I had been reading about the Upton Chamber for years and I was so excited to finally go inside. However, I hadn't gone more than one step when I turned and said, "Uh, oh."

Stepping back out I informed Mike that the entranceway was flooded, and at a depth that would easily cover our shoes. It was difficult to see back into the chamber, but when Mike tossed a small pebble, we heard the telltale *bloop* sound, which indicated that the water was even deeper back there. We hadn't driven over three hours to be stopped now, but what were we to do?

When Cathy arrived, she saved the day, for me, at least, as she had brought an extra pair of rubber boots. Mike had to roll up his pant legs, take off his socks, and tie plastic bags around his shoes. If people only knew what actually goes into these research adventures!

Cathy skillfully led the way by moving from rock to rock along the walls, keeping her feet out of the water. I walked right in, but quickly realized the boots weren't totally watertight. Mike tried to balance on some rocks and just when it looked like he would remain high and dry, a sudden slip resulted in ice cold water up to the middle of his shins.

After slipping into the deep, icy water, Mike tries to straddle some rocks with one bag still tied over his shoe. That's dedication!

Cold, wet feet aside, we listened in fascination as Cathy talked about the chamber, the OSL testing, and the concerted efforts to study and preserve the site. It was remarkable to stand inside such an ancient structure and imagine the reverence and wonder the builders felt as they peered down the entranceway and watched the summer solstice sunset and the stars of the Pleiades dip below the stone mounds on Pratt Hill.

I was surprised to see a small hole at the top of the high ceiling, and Cathy said there is some debate as to whether or not to cover it. Was it an original feature, and if so, did it have some type of significant alignment?

She also pointed out a section of the wall in the back where the stones were unusually jumbled. There is some oral history and written documentation (a letter from former resident Malcolm Pearson) that a second chamber adjoined this one, and "some recent scientific work showed that sunlight reflecting off the water in this chamber could have extended the light reflection period and may have illuminated the second chamber." No sign of the second chamber has yet been found, however, and it may have been removed by a farmer, if it ever existed.

The jumbled stones in the back wall.

Unfortunately, as much as I would have liked to stay inside longer, my feet had become completely numb and I was starting to shiver, and Mike certainly was doing no better. While I was able to dry off and put my socks and shoes back on, there was no way Mike could hike up Pratt Hill in the cold weather with soaked shoes. A detour to the local Wal-Mart got him some new hiking shoes and warm socks, and we were soon ascending Pratt Hill. And it was only then that Cathy told us the story of previous events here concerning a proposed cell tower, before the land was rescued by the ownership of the Narragansett Trust.

"A mapping by the FCC was requested by regional Tribes, Mashpee Wampanoag, Wampanoag Tribe of Gay Head (Aquinnah), and the Narragansett Tribe, to determine the best location of the cell tower that would not block the ceremonial alignment to the entranceway of the chamber at Heritage Park. At this point, the previous owner dismantled some of the features on top of the hill. There are no plans to rebuild the destroyed features, as cultural tradition tells us the stone groupings were made as prayers of stone and are not able to be rebuilt.

"From the mapping came a finding of eligibility for the National Register of Historic Places, and a non-contiguous district with the chamber at Heritage Park was established. The owner subsequently apologized for the removal of some of the features in a public meeting and offered the land for sale for purposes of preservation. Later, the Narragansett Trust purchased the land. The Narragansett Trust has plans for Pratt Hill to be an educational center to explain the importance of identification, protection, and preservation of ceremonial stone landscapes and features."

This case illustrates the importance of everyone working together within communities to bring awareness to such sites. While it is unfortunate some destruction occurred, the important thing is that now these sites are protected. And the stories of Pratt Hill and the Upton Chamber—as well as other sites throughout the Hudson Valley and the Northeast—will continue as further research is conducted, and we may all finally understand the meaning and value of these ceremonial landscapes.

For the last two years the Upton Historical Commission has had programs about the chamber for MA Archaeology Month. For more information see the town website under "Historical Commission." The Narragansett Trust is a non-profit organization dedicated to the preservation of land with ceremonial stone landscapes.

Heritage Park is located between 18 and 20 Elm Street, Upton, Massachusetts.

Interior of a chamber on Ninham Mountain, NY. Note the massive roof slabs and partial bench in the back. This chamber has an equinox sunrise alignment.

Calendar Sites

"Calendar site" is a term that describes any site that is used to mark time. In the Hudson Valley and northern New Jersey, such sites could contain walls, perched boulders, cairns, standing stones, or chambers, or any combination of any or all of them.

These stone features can have astronomical alignments to solstice and equinox sunrises and sunsets, the rising and setting of certain stars or constellations, or important lunar alignments. Such alignments can occur in a variety of ways, such as by light entering a chamber, a shadow cast by a standing stone, a line of sight along a wall or between a row of cairns or boulders, or between a single boulder and a mountain peak or valley on the horizon. A calendar site may have just one of these features and alignments on a small patch of ground, or it could have numerous alignments and features stretching across hundreds of acres.

The point is, that while calendar sites come in many shapes and sizes, they all have a common purpose—to tell what time of the year it is. *This is a basic human need* in parts of the world subject to changing seasons. In fact, survival depends upon knowing when it is warm enough to plant, when migrating wild game will be available, and when it is time to head south or build sturdy shelters for winter.

It should come as no surprise that people in the Hudson Valley built calendar sites. What would be astonishing is if they *didn't*.

Stone Walls

There is an old saying that familiarity breeds contempt. Such is the case with the ubiquitous stone walls of the Hudson Valley and New England—they are so numerous that residents don't pay much attention to them.

Of course, many of these stone walls don't deserve much attention, as they are just old boundary markers or served some other mundane purpose to farmers or the landowners. Yet, more people should pay attention to those unusual walls of extraordinary size, the walls that are astronomically aligned, or those that don't seem to serve any discernible purpose, especially on land unsuitable for farming. They should also pay attention to the incredible amount of walls that were catalogued back in 1871 in the Department of Agriculture's report *Statistics of Fences in the United States.*

For starters, it's amazing that anybody bothered to conduct such a bizarre survey, but I'm glad they did as the results were eye-opening. In her book *Sermons in Stone*[1], author Susan Allport wrote:

"The results of the survey are astounding. In 1871 approximately 1/3 of Connecticut's fences were made of stone, amounting to 20,505 miles of stonewall—enough to extend almost one time around the equator. Most of Rhode Island's 14,030 miles were stone, as were nearly half of Massachusetts' 32,960 miles. In New York, 18% of the fences were made of stone, a staggering 95,364 miles, more miles than there are in the coastline of the entire United States. Taken together, the states of New England and New York had more miles of stone walls than the United States has miles of railroad. The work that went into them, according to one estimate, would have built the pyramids of Egypt over 100 times over.

"It would have taken 1,000 men working 365 days a year about 59 years to build all the stone walls of Connecticut and 15,000 men 243 years to build the 252,539 miles of walls in New England and New York."

Take a moment to think about this. According to these calculations, from the period of 1628 to 1871, a dedicated labor force of 15,000 men would have had to have been working every day of the year to build the more than a quarter of a million miles of stone fence—which, by the way, would be more than long enough to stretch to the moon! While Allport writes that she is "increasingly resentful" of the suggestions that all the walls weren't built by colonial and postcolonial farmers, she also somewhat contradicts her own view by pointing out the following:

"What is well documented are the chronic labor shortages of the Colonies. From the beginning, these shortages were an inevitable and serious result of the cheapness of land, the lack of a permanent class of agricultural laborers (as existed in England), and the small amount of overseas immigration from 1675 to 1775."

---

[1] *Sermons in Stone, The Stone Walls of New England and New York*, Susan Allport, WW Norton & Company, NY 1990.

So, if there was such a "chronic labor shortage," how were hundreds of thousands of miles of walls built during that span of time? Couldn't some of these walls have already existed when the colonists arrived? Were the Native Americans so inept and useless that they were incapable of carrying stones and placing them on top of one another to make walls? I don't think so!

In fact, Allport also quotes several early sources that state that Native Americans "were remarkable for their excellence of their stone walls." For example:

"In 1677, the missionary Daniel Cookin noted that the Narragansett and Warrick tribes of Connecticut and Rhode Island were 'an active, laborious, and ingenious people which is demonstrated in their labors they do for the English of whom more are employed, especially in making stone fences and many other hard labors, than any other Indian people or neighbors.' "

So what are we to make of all this information? Who is right, or is everybody wrong? Once again, the problem lies between the staunch battle lines that are constantly being drawn in the stone sites war. There are those that insist that *every inch* of stone walls is the work of colonial and postcolonial farmers, or at least their slaves or hired help. Then there are those, as Allport states with dismay, "who contend that certain stone walls were built by much earlier visitors from Europe—Celts or Irish monks perhaps—who, they believe, established settlements in New England more than one thousand years ago."

Why are the Native Americans, who lived here for thousands of years, constantly being left out of the equation? Early colonists themselves stated that the local Indians—both men and women—were excellent stone wall builders. Couldn't their skills have been so good, because Native Americans had already been building in stone for generations?

With an astonishing 252,539 miles of stone walls in New York and New England, I think it is pushing the limits of credibility that they were solely the work of colonial and postcolonial farmers. On the other hand, while the idea of Celts or Irish monks building some walls a thousand years ago is an exciting concept, the idea is big on imagination and short on evidence—although I'm not willing to rule out the possibility of pre-Columbian European travel to North America.

In my opinion, some of these walls were built by Native Americans before the colonists arrived, and they were built for both the mundane purposes of farming or boundaries, as well as for astronomical or ceremonial purposes. And I continue to be amazed that this would be such a controversial idea with mainstream historians and archaeologists. There is this pervasive bias against Native Americans in the Northeast—and indeed, there has been since the Pilgrims landed at Plymouth Rock—in which they are viewed as having been incapable of having the brains and physical ability to build something simple like a stone wall, let along an astronomically aligned complex of walls, chambers, and cairns.

If nothing else, I hope this book will get people thinking, why not the Native Americans?

Indian Hill
Southfields, NY

Thanks to historian Doc Bayne, I learned about the strange walls at Indian Hill, which is part of Sterling Forest State Park. In November of 2013, Doc, Town of Chester historian Cliff Patrick—who mapped the site—and some other history buffs and I hiked to the walls of Indian Hill.

Along the way, Doc displayed an uncanny ability to spot where typical old farm walls and foundations stood. I wondered how the "massive walls"—as they are labeled on Patrick's map—differed, and would I be able to tell the difference? I needn't have wondered. These walls are huge, unmistakable, and inexplicable in terms of ordinary farm life, with some sections measuring as much as *twenty-four feet wide and over five feet high.*

There are several massive walls on this site, most notably a pair that run parallel for about half a mile. Would a simple stretch of country road, far from any town, seemingly going to nowhere, require such an enormous undertaking—on both sides of the road—to mark its path? And why do several other massive, single walls stick out from this double-walled lane, four of which run for about 270 feet and then just stop, some at the base of steep hills?

Just as remarkable is what appears to be the largest stone pile I've ever seen at any of these sites, measuring at least 25 feet high, and about

183 feet long (photo below). And it happens to stand just beyond an opening in one of the massive walls, and near one of those single walls on the other side of the lane. Perhaps this hill of stones was deposited by a glacier, as it is absurd to think it is the result of a farmer clearing a field, carrying large rocks up to such a height.

I could not find any articles or papers published on the massive walls and stone pile at Indian Hill, which is probably due to the fact that conventional thought views these features as just part of an old farming community. Some have even suggested these massive walls played a role in the Southfields Furnace, but the furnace is a mile to the south, so it is highly unlikely there is any connection, and there is certainly no obvious purpose for them.

I wasn't sure what to think of Indian Hill, and went back again and again to study the landscape, hoping that the key to unlocking some of the mysteries here would once again be astronomical alignments. Were there any alignments relating to the massive stone walls? If so, then the scales would tip strongly away from any colonial origins and toward Native Americans, or some other ancient people.

Using Cliff Patrick's map, I placed my solstice/equinox template over various points along the massive walls. Lo and behold, right away I found that a straight, 270-foot section of wall, jutting from the south side of the double-walled lane, pointed to the important winter solstice sunrise! Of course, one alignment does not make a calendar site, but perhaps four important alignments do, which is exactly what I discovered. About 500 feet from this winter solstice sunrise wall is another massive 270-foot wall, on the north side of the double-walled lane, which points to summer solstice sunset!

Map of Indian Hill Massive Walls, South Fields, NY
Linda Zimmermann 2016
Based on GPS measurements from Garmin Oregon 450t
and survey map by Cliff Patrick
Not to scale N

353°

173°

Massive Single Wall ~ 270', Width ~ 13.5', Height ~ 5'

Massive Wall is in 3 sections

Massive Wall in two equal sections, overall ~270' long

353°

173°

~20' wide at this point

White Line Indicates Massive Double-Walled Lane

30'±

Oriented toward Winter Solstice Sunrise & Summer Solstice Sunset

Oriented toward Winter Solstice Sunrise & Summer Solstice Sunset

302°

Massive Single Wall ~270' long

~270' long, 5' high, gets wider at end

4' wide

Ends at base of hill

Scientific & Summer Solstice Sunset

Large boulders visible at top of hill

Massive Single Wall

Rock Pile ~193' long, ~35' high

To Summer Solstice Sunrise & Winter Solstice Sunset

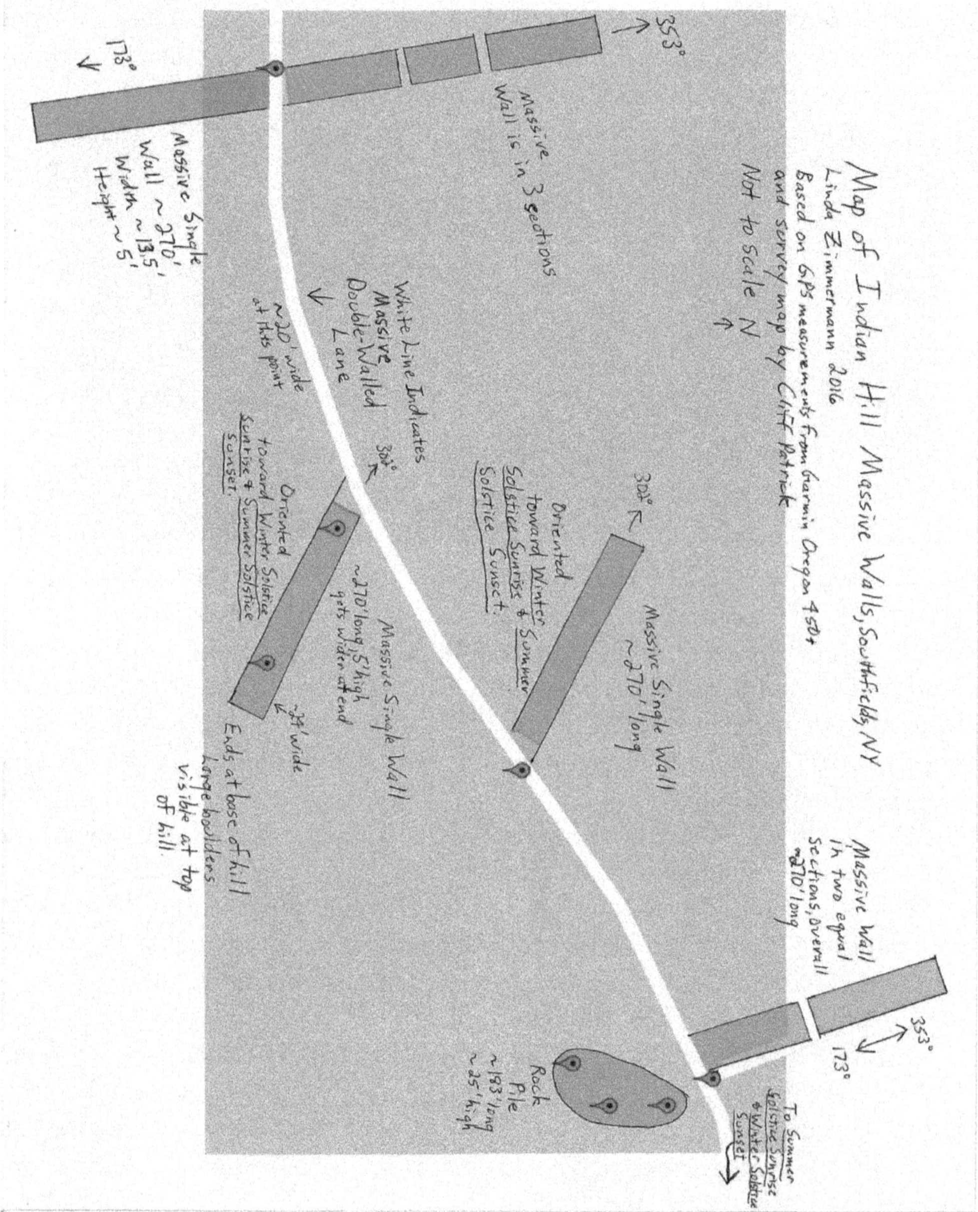

And another 500 feet beyond that, there is a fairly straight section of the double-walled lane that runs for about 500 feet. People standing

between those walls on the first day of summer, looking down that road to the northeast, would be looking directly at where the sun rises. And if they were to be standing there facing the other direction down the road in late December, they would see the winter solstice sunset.

The end of the double-walled lane oriented to summer solstice sunrise
and winter solstice sunset.

This would all be a remarkable coincidence if these adjacent features were aligned with the four solstice sunrises and sunsets purely by accident!

In February of 2016, Bob and I returned to take more measurements, coordinates, and check the alignments and horizon views. Here are my observations from that day:

- What I believed to be the Winter Solstice Sunrise wall gets wider toward the end, to an impressive 24 feet. Curiously, it just ends at the base of a steep hill. I did observe some large boulders on top of the hill which could possibly be used as alignment markers. Still, it seemed to be a strange way to observe a sunrise at the base of a hill, so it dawned on me that perhaps I was looking at it wrong—180 degrees wrong. As the same line that points to Winter Solstice Sunrise also points to Summer Solstice Sunset in the other direction, perhaps that was the purpose of this wall?

- Just about 500 feet away from this wall is what I had called the Summer Solstice Sunset wall, and indeed, it is oriented to

302 degrees. Of course, as stated above, it also could point to Winter Solstice Sunrise in the opposite direction. The point is, that there are two sections of massive walls, both about 270 feet long, and both oriented in the same direction, which both happen to point to an important solstice sunrise and solstice sunset. To my way of thinking, that is beyond coincidence and ridiculous to think a farmer did this by accident. It is intentional and with exacting purpose.

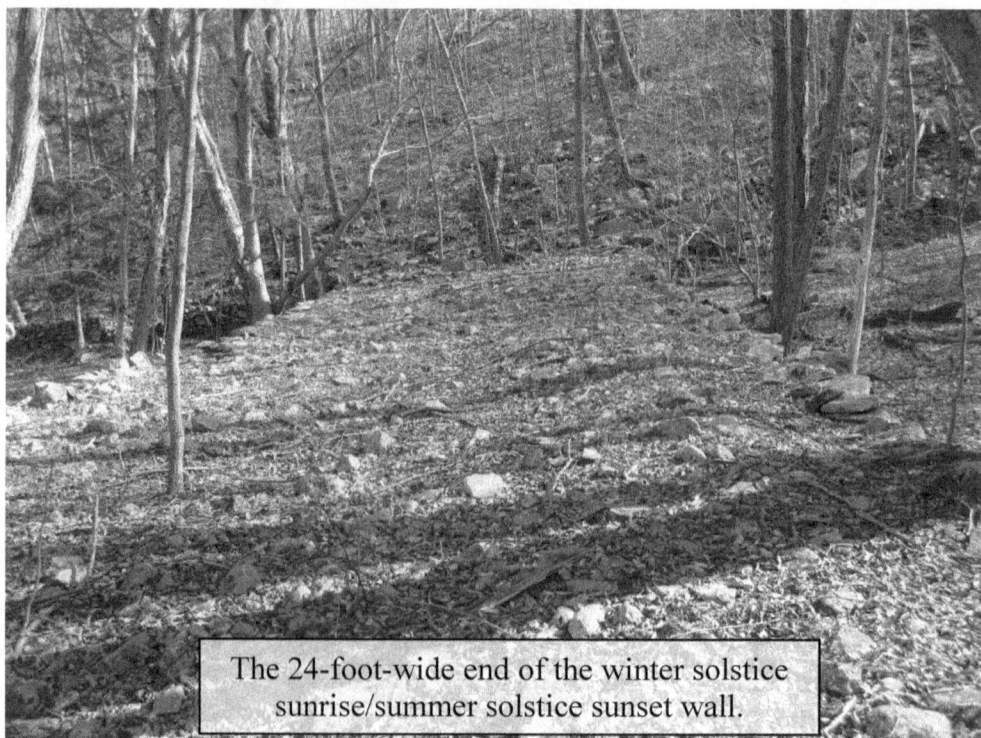

The 24-foot-wide end of the winter solstice sunrise/summer solstice sunset wall.

- At the end of the double-walled lane by a stream, I used the GPS unit's 3-D viewing function, and I was able to "see" the horizon despite all of the trees. There is a double-peaked hill and curved depression in the direction of summer solstice sunrise. Direct observation—if possible—or more precise mapping and measurements are required to determine over which of these features the sun actually rises on the first day of summer.

The virtual 3D view of the horizon where summer solstice sunrise would occur.

- The enormous stone pile is quite strange. Is it a natural hill that was covered with rocks, or is it all a huge pile of rocks? Some of the rocks along the sides are very large and rough, while on top it seems to be mostly smaller, more rounded stones. From the top, you get an excellent view of the double-walled lane just below, and one of the single sections of wall on the north side of the lane which points to 353 degrees. It is also by two of the openings to the lane, and by a stream.

Stone Pile

North Wall

- Just to play devil's advocate, the four sections of wall that I measured to be about 270 feet long, may in fact be 100 megalithic yards, or 272 feet. As mentioned in the last chapter, the megalithic yard is a controversial unit of measurement proposed by Alexander Thom. He believed that over 600 megalithic sites in Europe used this unit of measurement.

- Two sections of massive walls on the north side of the double-walled lane are both oriented to 353 degrees and 173 degrees. I will be researching the possibilities of these directions having some astronomical significance, but again, would two walls be oriented the same by accident? And they would be poor boundary markers as they just end, with no fourth connecting wall to mark a boundary.

- There is a lot of water at this site in the form of swamps and streams, and some of the walls and their openings seem to be related. On that warm day in February of 2016, sections of the lane between the double walls were more of a lake than a road. One stream has what Cliff Patrick called a weir (photo below), a type of low stone dam used to trap fish. This weir is located near the stone pile and at the east end of the lane.

- In terms of the massive walls with astronomical alignments, I think this is another site that existed before the colonists arrived. Later farmers probably tried to utilize the walls and lane for their purposes, and more recent features were then added to the landscape. I know I keep repeating myself, but the thought that farmers would move such massive quantities of stone and create astronomical alignments just for fun or by accident is just beyond reason.

It's very exciting to think that I might be the first person in modern times to see an astronomical connection here, but I realize that further research is clearly needed to study the site to confirm my theory and look for other possible alignments. Are there boulders or other features to mark the equinoxes? Does the massive stone pile play a role in any alignments? Why did the builders choose this site; is it somehow connected to other calendar sites? And, of course, maps, coordinates, and templates are all well and good, but direct observation is the best way to uncover and confirm any possible alignments.

Indian Hill, with its massive stone walls, is a remarkable site that may have been part of yet another Native American ceremonial landscape. The more one hikes the woods of the Hudson Valley—keeping a sharp eye and open mind—the more these sites are coming to light. While in many places a rock wall is just a rock wall, at Indian Hill it can be something truly extraordinary.

One final observation: While plotting some points after writing this section, I found that the Lake Tiorati calendar site is just 3.6 miles to the east of Indian Hill. The Ramapo Walls are only 7.94 miles to the south of Indian Hill, making all of these sites within a day's walk from each other.

Warning: Hunting is allowed here, so please check with the Sterling Forest State Park office for the latest schedule. I have been here a couple of times during hunting season, and it is rather disconcerting to be trying to take measurements and check for astronomical alignments with guns firing around you. It's always best to wear a brightly-colored jacket and hat, or a safety vest, as even in the off-season, I have encountered hunters in the woods at various locations.

Directions: On Orange Turnpike in Southfields, at coordinates N 41.261526, W 074.182684, look for the Indian Hill sign. Drive up a fairly rough dirt road to the parking area. There is metal gate at the trail head. Go up the hill beyond the gate and then follow the yellow trail markers, which will lead you to the massive stone walls. If you are navigating with a GPS unit, one of the solstice walls is at: N 41.26518, W 074.16850.

The end of the south wall of the double-walled lane, above. Below, Bob captures the moment I confirm my theory that one of the walls was oriented toward summer solstice sunset.

The Basics of Astronomical Alignments

When looking for astronomical alignments at a stone site, I created a template similar to this which shows the general positions on the horizon where solstice and equinox sunrises and sunsets would occur for the Hudson Valley, as well as the positons of the maximum and minimum Moon risings and settings for the 18.6 year cycle.

Using programs online such as www.suncalc.net, you can see the exact sun rising and setting positions for any location and any day.

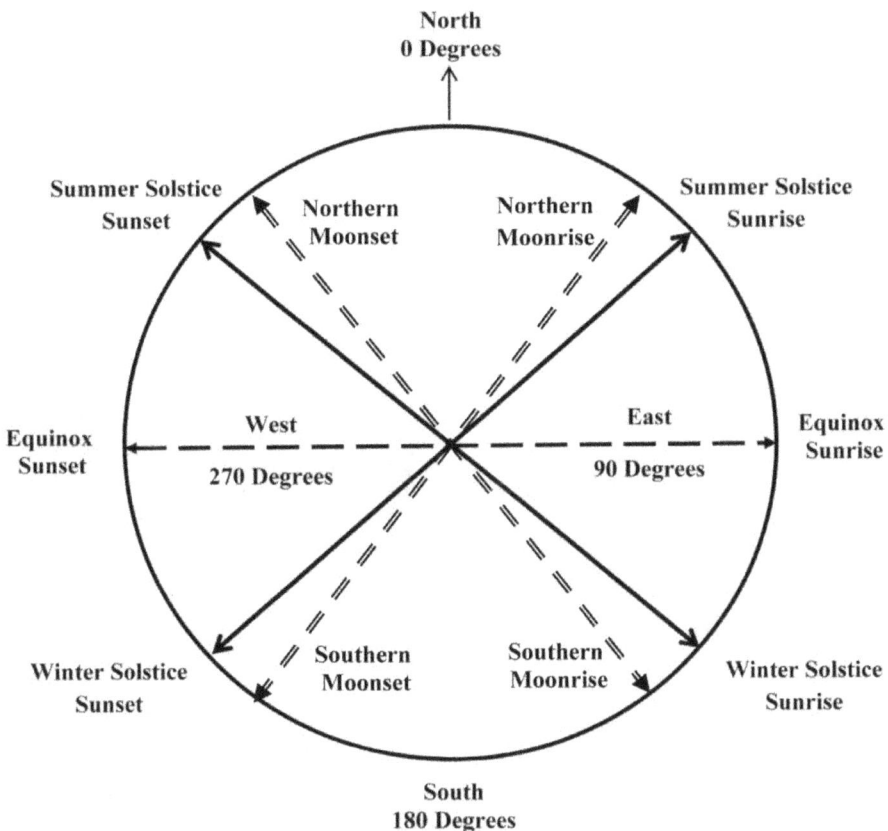

Note: If using an electronic device to determine compass headings, make sure you have the unit set for True North. Due to the earth's magnetic field, the readings you get from a standard compass will be off by an average of about 12.5 degrees in the Hudson Valley. This deviation is known as magnetic declination.

Magnetic declination is very important for a number of reasons:

- If you are trying to navigate through the woods with a standard compass and don't know the magnetic declination for your location, you will quickly get lost.
- If you are trying to determine astronomical alignments and aren't aware of the magnetic declination, you will overlook them all because you will be about 12.5 degrees off.

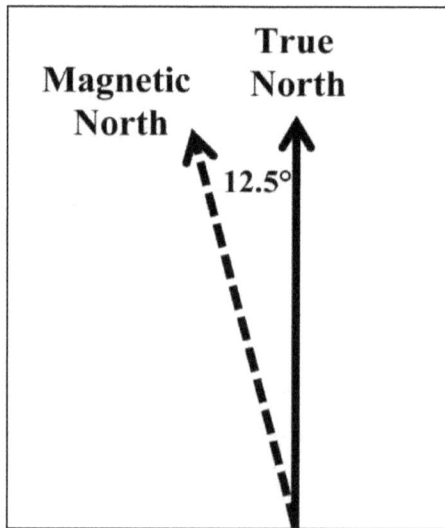

To determine the exact magnetic declination for any location, go to:
http://www.ngdc.noaa.gov/geomag-web/#declination

The easiest thing to do is get a compass app for your smartphone. If you will be somewhere that there won't be any cell service, get a dedicated GPS hiking unit, preferably with installed topographic maps.

Once you have obtained coordinates, measurements, and compass headings at a stone site, websites such as www.stellarium.org will help chart the movements of the sun, Moon, and stars to look for possible alignments.

Lake Tiorati
Harriman State Park, New York

In the early stages of my research, I spoke with Thomas Brannan, who is a member of the Orange County Chapter of the New York State Archaeological Association. As an engineer and land surveyor for over 30 years, he learned "to distinguish quite easily between natural formations of stones as they were distributed by the great glaciers, and man-made landmarks."[2]

He told me about the High Point site (described later in this chapter), and also about a stone calendar site overlooking Lake Tiorati in Harriman State Park, in Orange County, New York. This came as a great surprise, because when I was a child, my family and I made frequent trips to the lake for boating and fishing. In my teens, I also began hiking extensively throughout Harriman State Park, yet I never heard about this calendar site which sat right along the Appalachian Trail.

---

[2] *Orange County Historical Society Journal*, V15, November 1986

The very next day, my husband, Bob, and I, headed for Lake Tiorati, and parked in the lot by the traffic circle. A short walk up the steep road going west from the Tiorati traffic circle brings you to the Appalachian Trail. Before heading south on the trail, we came upon a colorful character who called himself Dixie Grits. He was from Alabama and had already hiked 1,300 miles of the 2,168 mile-long trail stretching from Springer Mountain, Georgia, to Mount Katahdin in Maine. Dixie was not a young man, by any means, and I asked why he had chosen to do this at his age.

"Because I was pissed off that I turned 60!" he said with a smile and that distinctive Alabama accent.

We wished him the best of luck on his journey, told him to keep an eye out for stone sites, and then we parted ways. (As a side note, thanks to Dixie, I bought a pair of similar Black Diamond hiking poles that he used, which I now can't live without. You never know who you will meet or what you will learn on a hike!)

I was concerned that we wouldn't be able to find the calendar site in a landscape full of rocks, with only a general idea of its location. After about half a mile, I was really getting worried, but then I had to laugh when the huge perched boulder presented itself right next to the trail. If you decide to go to this site, don't worry, you *can't* miss it.

It is indeed an impressive, arrowhead-shaped, perched boulder that stands about 7 feet high, is 19 feet long, and is 13 feet at the widest part. There are numerous other smaller boulders within sight of this large one, and I really had to give credit to Tom Brannan and his team for making sense of it all by thoroughly mapping the site in 1980 and finding numerous solar alignments in the process.

However, even if the perched boulder was the only feature here, it would still be a significant site, as Brannan's team found that by standing behind the flat, eastern side of the boulder, one could watch summer solstice sunrise over a 3-foot-high rock about 162 feet away.

This was fascinating, but I wondered why the pointed end of the boulder wasn't aiming toward the winter solstice. There also weren't any notations on Brannan's map as to any possible alignments in the direction it was pointing. After creating a solstice and equinox template for this location's coordinates using SunCalc.net, I superimposed it on the site map and found that the perched boulder actually appeared to be pointing directly to the winter solstice sunset! Of course, I would need to observe the exact position of the sun around December 21-22 to see if this was accurate.

Unfortunately, for many seasons in a row, my repeated attempts to actually view the winter solstice sunset (as well as any equinox alignments) were all met with cloud cover or rain. It really made me wonder how many years it took the builders of these calendar sites to perfect their alignments, given the propensity for bad weather in the Northeast!

Finally, on Friday, December 18, 2015, both opportunity and weather appeared ready to cooperate. After weeks of wonderfully mild temperatures, however, a chilling cold had arrived, accompanied by strong winds. I confess I wasn't the happiest camper as we hiked up to the Tiorati site, sucking frigid air into my lungs, but observing an "almost solstice sunset" would be worth the discomfort.

Then, just minutes after we arrived, clouds rolled in—and just along the western horizon! It was clear everywhere else, but the god of weather seemed determined to keep us from seeing the setting sun. We waited anyway, and the brightest region of the clouds gave some indication that the huge perched boulder could be in a winter solstice alignment, but it certainly wasn't conclusive.

Two days later on December 20, Bob and I were up at 4:45am (after a big Zimmermann family Christmas party the night before, no less!) to hike to the Whangtown Road chamber to watch "almost solstice sunrise." The weather was mostly clear and the trip was a complete success, but we were really beat by the time we got home. Despite our lack of sleep and fatigue, however, with the 21st and 22nd forecast to be cloudy and rainy, the prospect of clear skies at the Tiorati site for sunset that night was too tempting to resist, so we went back out for our second hike of the day.

My hiking boots felt a bit like lead weights as I trudged onward and upward once again. We arrived early enough that we could explore more of the other stones in the site. As sunset approached, however, all eyes were on the triangular perched boulder—and the thin strip of clouds that suddenly manifested on the western horizon. I believe I muttered a less polite version of "Oh no, you don't!" and hoped the sun would reappear beneath the line of clouds before it was too late.

Fortunately, the sun did reemerge from under the clouds about ten minutes before sunset, but then to my disappointment, I realized that there was no way the perched boulder would point exactly to the spot on the horizon were the sun would set, as the tip of the rock was aimed a little further west. Had the boulder slipped out of position on the inclined bedrock in the 35 years since the site survey had been taken? Or, had the small scale of the drawing simply only made it appear to be in a direct line for winter solstice sunset?

Anxious minutes ticked by, until I decided to stand on what Brannan and his team had determined to be the "Apparent Observation Point" for the entire site, where equinox and summer solstice alignments could be observed with the large rocks in the surrounding landscape. Orienting myself with the distinct boulder in the distance which was used to observe the equinox sunrises, I then turned toward the perched boulder and observed the orange sphere of the setting sun cradled nicely in the center of the curved depression along the top edge on the back side!

Of course, given any set of rocks and features, one can find some sort of alignments, but as I was standing right on the suspected observation spot viewing this, I couldn't help thinking that this winter solstice sunset alignment was significant. It does seem more likely than not, at a place where at least a dozen large rocks had been carefully positioned into a calendar site, that this perched boulder would play some role in determining another important time of the year.

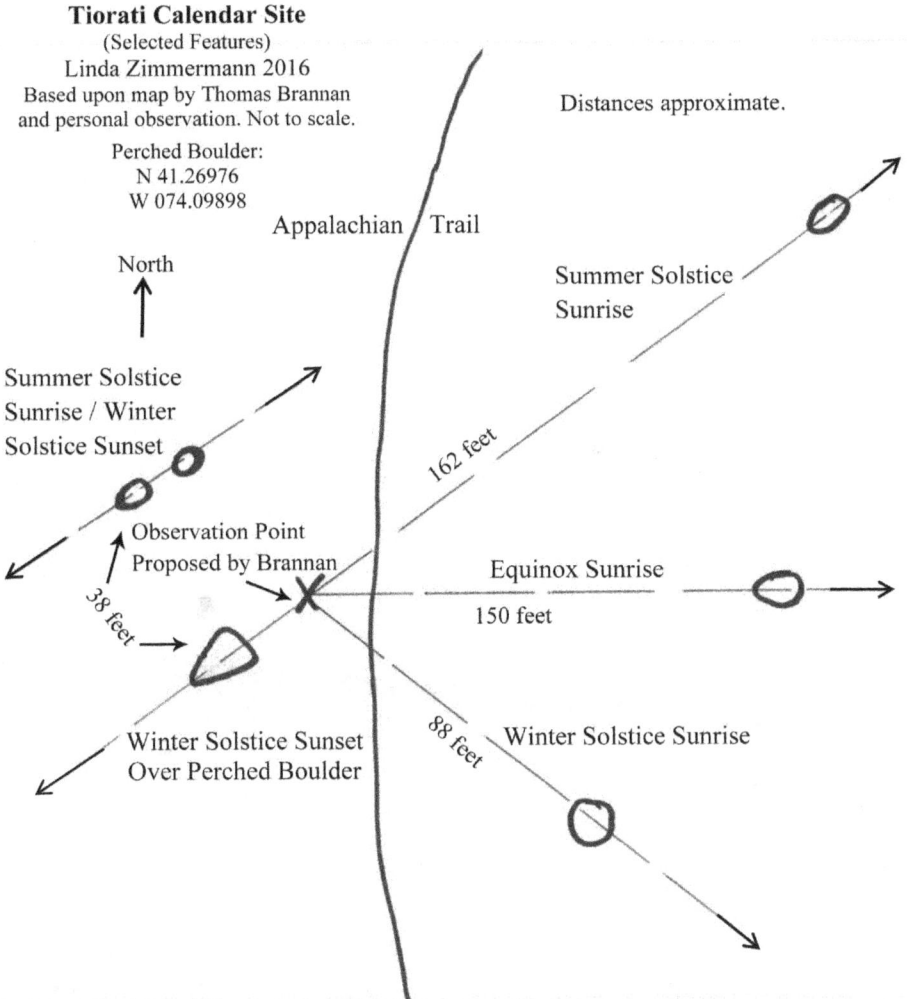

Tiorati Calendar Site
(Selected Features)
Linda Zimmermann 2016
Based upon map by Thomas Brannan
and personal observation. Not to scale.

Distances approximate.

Perched Boulder:
N 41.26976
W 074.09898

Appalachian / Trail

Summer Solstice
Sunrise

North

Summer Solstice
Sunrise / Winter
Solstice Sunset

162 feet

Observation Point
Proposed by Brannan

Equinox Sunrise

150 feet

38 feet

Winter Solstice Sunset
Over Perched Boulder

88 feet

Winter Solstice Sunrise

In fact, Brannan and his team recognized that some of the solstice and equinox alignments had been duplicated around the site, leading them to surmise that there may have been several phases in the construction of this calendar site. For example, they identified at least three sets of boulders which all pointed to the summer solstice sunrise. Had several generations of builders added their own alignments to this site? How many years had it taken to build, and how many years was it in use?

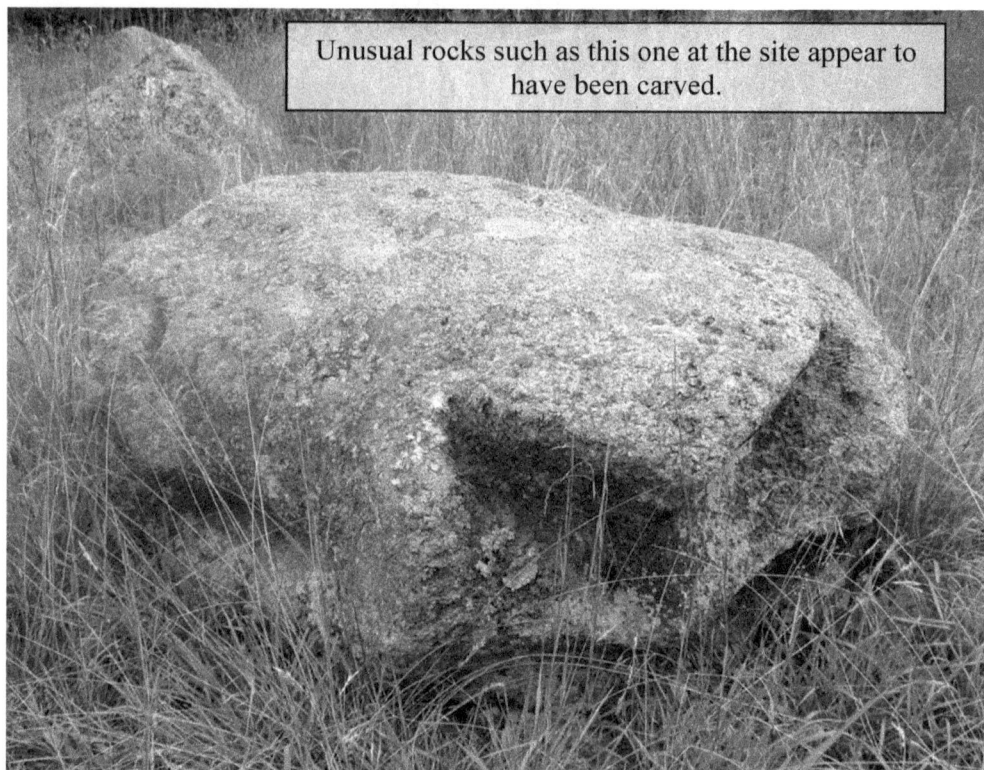

Unusual rocks such as this one at the site appear to have been carved.

The biggest questions, again, are when was it built and who were these builders? It doesn't make sense that early colonists would have spent the time and effort pushing rocks around a hilltop to determine what season it was, when there were printed calendars, churches, and courts that could all tell you the exact day of the year. I think local Native Americans are the obvious choice as the builders of this site, and many other calendar sites throughout the Northeast. There will no doubt be speculation that it could have been some Pre-Columbian European culture that aligned these stones, but there is currently no proof of that, nor any compelling reason to even think in that direction, when there were indigenous people who were certainly watching the skies and were capable of moving rocks.

Regardless of who you think may have built this site, it is still another hidden gem in the Hudson Valley landscape worthy of recognition, preservation, and additional research.

Additional Observation:

On December 18, 2015, as we waited for sunset, Bob noticed what looked to be drill holes in one of the rocks near the observation point. I had seen circular holes in rocks at other sites, but this one was unusual as it appeared to have a triangular-shaped hole, as well. As the triangle appeared to be aimed at one of the circles, I decided to see what direction it was pointing. My Garmin GPS unit gave me a heading of 302 degrees, which at this location happens to be where the summer solstice sunset would occur! This seemed to be too much to be a coincidence at a location with proven solar alignments.

The rock also has another circular hole to the left, and a grooved channel runs between the two circular holes. There is also an irregular, elongated indentation to the bottom right. The rock has white quartz crystals protruding from the surface, and natural weathering can cause crystal formations to fall out, and further weathering may make the resulting holes look man-made. Whether completely caused by weathering, completely man-made, or a combination of the two, this is a most interesting rock.

Also, in 2014, *Orange Magazine* asked to interview me and they wondered if there was a unique location I could suggest for my photo shoot for the article. I immediately suggested the Tiorati perched boulder, if their photographer for was up for a hike.

Much to my delight, the photographer was Erik Gliedman, whose work I admired due to his fabulous creative use of lighting, and fortunately he was ready for an adventure. What I didn't realize was how much heavy gear he had to carry. Feeling somewhat guilty, I shouldered some of the weight on our hike.

It was kind of a surreal experience for me, as I hiked to the site in my favorite Vasque hiking boots and long pants, and then went behind the boulder to change into a skirt and heels. In the midst of the shoot, a lone hiker passed by and was clearly puzzled as to why a man was taking pictures of a woman in a skirt and heels in the middle of the woods. I simply smiled at him and enigmatically said, "Don't ask."

I was thrilled to see the results of Erik's efforts that day, and his photos of me at the Tiorati site are among my favorites. Not only did his lighting techniques cast the perfect shadows and highlights on the rock, he was he even able to make me look good!

Erik's website: http://www.erikchristianphotography.com/

Directions to Lake Tiorati Site: At the north end of Lake Tiorati in Harriman State Park, there is a traffic circle where Seven Lakes Drive meets Tiorati Brook Road and Arden Valley Road in Southfields, NY. There is a parking lot there, and they do charge a fee depending upon the season. Walk west on Arden Valley Road until you come to the Appalachian Trail at the top of the hill. Turn left and follow the trail uphill to the coordinates of the huge perched boulder: N41.26975 W074.09890. If you do not have a GPS device, don't worry, you can't miss it as it is right next to the trail. The total distance from the parking lot to the site is 0.8 miles.

Photo courtesy of Erik Gliedman

Last Minute Addition

I did not expect to be writing anything about the equinox sunrise of Sunday, March 20, 2016, as for about a week before, weather forecasters were calling for a major Nor'easter with 5 to 12 inches of snow expected around the area. By Friday, however, those snow totals dropped to just a dusting to a few inches, and on Saturday there were even indications that there might actually be a few hours of only partly cloudy skies for Sunday at dawn. Would I finally get a chance to view an equinox sunrise at a calendar site?

When the alarm went off at 5am Sunday morning, I opened a window and stuck out my head –stars were shining and there was not a cloud in the sky! Bob and I hurried to get dressed and skipped breakfast to make sure we wouldn't be late. Unfortunately, the recent warm weather had been replaced by the low twenties, and the thirty-minute hike in the darkness from the Lake Tiorati parking area up to the calendar site wasn't exactly fun.

We were both very excited, though, as a patch of sky on the eastern horizon brightened with reds and pinks. I stood at the observation point for the site, facing the equinox alignment boulder on the top of the ridge indicated by Brannan's map. Bob stood behind a rock that was supposed to line up with another rock on the ridge.

"There it is! It's starting!" I announced with great anticipation, as the bright, curved edge of the sun peeked over the horizon.

Within seconds, however, I was very concerned, as from the observation point near the huge perched boulder; I could not get a clear shot of the sun coming up over the equinox boulder because of all of the trees. Had I waited so many years, come up here in the cold and dark, for nothing?

Jumping to the right, I could clearly see the sun, but not the boulder. Shifting to my left, I could see the boulder, but the sun was obscured in the trees. Precious seconds ticked by as I started to run forward and back, left and right, trying to get that one photo that would forever confirm the equinox's alignment. Bob and I did the best we could, and then I started looking for other possible alignments on the hilltop.

I'm not exactly on line with the sun, boulder (see arrow) and
observation point, but this was the best I could do with all the trees.

82

I was standing behind the "carved" rock with the triangle and circle summer solstice sunset markings, facing east, when Bob told me to turn around. *Why on earth should I turn around*, I thought, when the sunrise was in front of me and the window of opportunity was closing as the sun rapidly ascended?

"*Just turn around*," he said with more urgency.

Spinning around, I saw the flat back of the perched boulder was illuminated by the orange light of the equinox sunrise, and my shadow was on the boulder. And there was another shadow being cast, as well, as the rounded, carved rock in front of me was casting a shadow into the curved, recessed, area of the boulder. Hurrying to the other side of that carved rock, I saw the beautiful sight of this carved rock bathed in orange light, casting shadows onto the orange glow on the boulder, but the sight didn't last long. Within minutes, the rising sun had lost its orange color, and the angle had shifted so that the rock and I were no longer creating shadows on the back of the boulder.

My heart sank when I converted this photo to black and white for the book, and the beautiful orange glow with my dark shadow faded to almost nothing. Though far less dramatic, you can still see the shadow of my body in the middle of the carved rock, and my head on the perched boulder. The shadow on the upper right of the perched boulder is from the trees; otherwise the entire back would have been illuminated.

This really demonstrated the importance of visiting these sites on the equinox, solstice, and other suspected celestial alignment dates. I hadn't even thought to look to the huge perched boulder for anything to do with the equinox, yet here was the most beautiful sight to be seen that morning. Anyone standing behind the carved rock on the first day of spring or fall would have no doubt what day it was, as the warm orange light of sunrise would cast their shadow onto the perched boulder for a few fleeting moments, making the observer part of the alignment. Given the numerous other alignments at this site, I did not think this was a coincidence.

A week earlier, I had been speaking at a local author's event at the Newburgh, New York library about the importance of research. I had alluded to how many miles I had hiked for this project—mostly uphill!—but said it was all worth it because going to these stone sites made the difference between simply rewriting other people's work, and making my own discoveries. I'm glad I listened to my own advice, as it was an amazing experience!

(And FYI, just a minute after I took my last photograph at the site, the clouds rolled in and covered the sun!)

I also predicted that equinox sunset would occur over this boulder on the ridge, and was happily able to confirm it during the fall equinox of 2016!

Ramapo Walls

I am nothing if not persistent. For many years, I had been trying to find the Ramapo Walls I read about, which had been depicted on an 1845 map in the collection of local resident Pierson Mapes. The map was entitled, "Supposed Prehistoric Walls on the 'Wrightman Fields' Ramapo, N.Y." Obviously, the key word here is "Prehistoric," so at the time this map was drawn, they must already have been considered to be very old, and important enough to take the time to survey and record them.

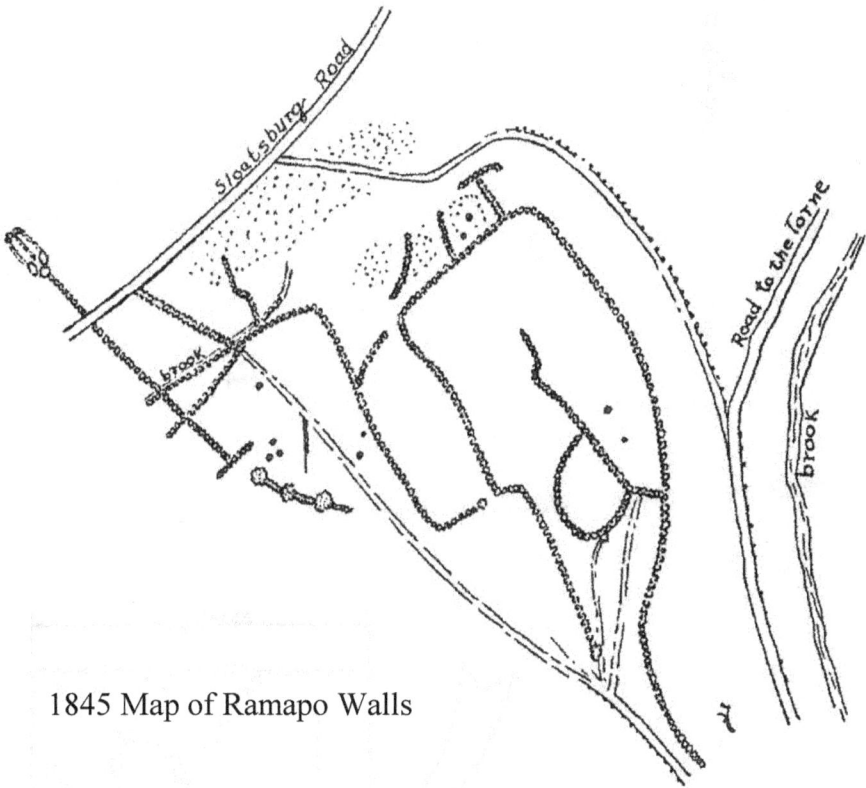

1845 Map of Ramapo Walls

The name "Ramapo Walls," however, does not fully convey the nature of this vast 200-acre site. In addition to the bizarre assortment of large and small walls that start and stop, and curve and bend, for no discernable reason, there are also sixteen stone cairns—enormous mounds of rock as large as *sixty* feet in diameter and *eight* feet high—as well as several large boulders dotting the landscape. It is a puzzling collection of features, but fortunately, we can get a much clearer view of the stone complex thanks to the combined work of the New Jersey Highlands Historical Society and NEARA, who in 1969 began a four-year study and survey of the site, and whose findings were summarized in an article with an excellent map by historian Edward Lenik, reproduced below with his permission.[3]

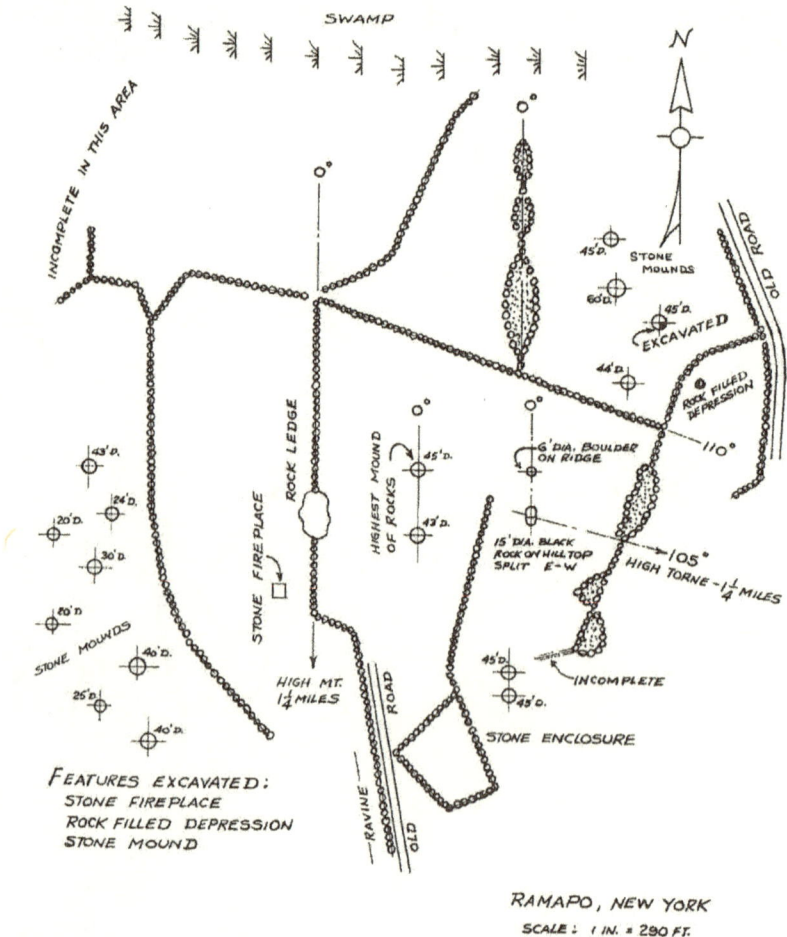

RAMAPO, NEW YORK
SCALE: 1 IN. = 280 FT.

---

[3] Their work is presented in the article *The Riddle of the Prehistoric Walls, Ramapo, New York*, by Edward Lenik in *The Bulletin*, the publication of The New York State Archaeological Association, Number 63, March, 1975, pages 1-14.

The goal of the project was to try to find out who built the site, when, and why. There have been numerous theories as to the origins, but even after four years of study, the team generated no definitive proof to back any claim. Examining each of these theories will help to get a better idea of how this location has been viewed over the years.

One of the 16 large cairns on the site.

One of the explanations put forth for the site was that it was the result of "busy work" or defensive fortifications made by American troops during the Revolutionary War. Soldiers were indeed posted at "Fort Sidman" two miles to the south, which was described as simply being a two-story blockhouse, and according to several reports, it was apparently in constant need of repair. Therefore, it is highly doubtful that instead of fortifying the blockhouse, which could save their lives if the British attacked, American soldiers were sent two miles away to the top of a hill to randomly pile stones which had no purpose. Clearly, this theory not only has no merit, it is totally absurd and can be dismissed outright.

At the other end of the spectrum, there is a theory that a pre-Columbian group of people, possibly Bronze Age Europeans, built the walls and cairns for ceremonial purposes. While this is a romantic notion for alternative history enthusiasts, no artifacts have as yet been uncovered at the site to support this idea.

The prevailing belief is that these stone walls are nothing more than the result of farmers clearing fields or creating boundary markers, and the massive stone mounds were also just the result of field clearing. From an agricultural perspective, the soil here appears thin and rocky; not conducive to farming. From an historic perspective, no one has yet to uncover who Wrightman was, and no farmhouse or barn remains have been found anywhere on the site.

If the walls were intended to be boundary markers, then they fail miserably to delineate or actually enclose any boundaries. Also, if they were the result of simple field clearing, this endeavor also failed, as the ground still remains littered with stones. If a farmer was going to undertake the incredible effort of constructing over a mile of walls and 16 massive piles of stones, why wouldn't he complete the task and actually *clear* the landscape? In my opinion, the farm theory is unreasonable and has no validity.

In terms of the idea that Native Americans may have constructed this site, there are several factors supporting this. For starters, they lived in the area for thousands of years. Rock shelters have been found nearby, as well as numerous Native American artifacts such as pottery, projectile points, and other signs of habitation, excavated by researcher and author Max Schrabisch in the early 20th century.

Unfortunately, for some reason, Native American stone construction of *anything* in the Northeast is an idea that is frowned upon, if not outwardly criticized. However, when contemplating what group of people had the time, opportunity, manpower, and motive for building the Ramapo walls and cairns, Native Americans should be at the top of the list—and perhaps the *only* ones on that list. Motive is the key to this site, but how can we hope to get into the minds of the builders with such a confusing array of features?

While I had the site map and article by Lenik, obviously the best way to make any determination about a location is to see it in person, which, as I alluded to at the beginning of this chapter, was a bit of a journey in itself. For a couple of years, a few local historians promised they would take me to the Ramapo Walls. Busy schedules, weather, and numerous other factors conspired to keep those plans from ever materializing.

Finally in July of 2013, I decided to try to find them on my own and started out with a friend, Susan Sciotto-Brown, on a hike from the Reeves

Meadow parking area on Seven Lakes Drive in Sloatsburg, NY. I had been told to follow certain trails for about two miles, but at some point we would have to turn onto some unmarked trails. When we came to the Ramapo Walls we "couldn't miss them"—unless the dense, summer undergrowth was hiding them. It all turned out to be a lovely hike on a beautiful day, but no walls or cairns were found.

I had also heard that the site was once identified as the "Circle of Stones" on older trail maps, and my husband, Bob, fortunately still had all of his hiking maps from the 1970s. There was the Circle of Stones marked on one of the maps, not far beyond a water tower at the end of Council Crest Road in Sloatsburg. We parked there and headed into the woods, determined to find this site. What we found was a labyrinth of unmarked trails and old roads going off in all directions. There were no walls or cairns to be seen that day, but we did come upon someone's recent artwork of an Easter Island figure.

Another historian had told me that the easiest way to find the site was to park on Torne Valley Road in Suffern, walk onto the New York State Thruway and head north to the restricted tractor trailer lot and road salt depot, climb over or under the fence, and then climb the mountain until I started seeing walls and cairns. In addition to this being highly dangerous (and probably illegal) to walk on the Thruway, there was the part about jumping a fence in a restricted area that had "getting arrested" written all over it.

However, at least now I knew just where the site was located (theoretically), and so I determined to park on Torne Valley Road and take the trail leading to the *Ramapo Powerlinez* rock climbing area and find the site from there. Bob and I were coming back from New Jersey late one Saturday afternoon in the fall of 2015, and decided to stop for a quick exploratory hike. We went far enough to believe that it was feasible, but fading light kept us from going further.

Later that fall, we set off early one morning from Torne Valley Road. We followed trails, we went off the trails and explored the woods, and finally came upon a line of huge electrical towers and thought that by following them, we would get to the site—but on another day, as we had tired by that point.

Yet another attempt brought us back to the electrical tower where we had stopped on the last hike, but to get to the next tower would involve going down a very steep slope of several hundred feet, then climbing up another steep slope of several hundred feet. (This route had "sprained ankle" written all over it.) We headed back into the woods for a while, hoping to find less treacherous terrain, but the steep ridge continued as far as we could see. We knew where we had to go, but it was like the old saying, "You can't get there from here." So close, yet so far.

One of the smartest things I did on any of my five unsuccessful attempts, was on the last hike I used my Garmin GPS unit to mark the coordinates of the electrical tower nearest the steep slope. That would enable me to use it as a reference point to navigate by if we once again tried the Council Crest/Water Tower parking as a starting point.

On Christmas Day in 2015, after Bob and I tore into our presents and had a hearty breakfast, we headed back to Council Crest Road, hoping that the sixth time was the charm. We parked in the small area at the end of the road, and programming in the electrical tower as my destination on the Garmin, I saw that our path would lead directly to the Circle of Stones indicated on the old map, as well as lead directly above the road salt depot on the Thruway. All indicators seemed to be converging on the elusive Ramapo Walls, and I was certain that years of effort were about to pay off.

However, Bob, with his self-professed "unerring and uncanny sense of direction," had other ideas. We originally agreed on the general direction to head out, but very shortly after, he began insisting on going left, even when all of the maps, coordinates, and my instincts said to go right. With every few steps, I wanted to continue to follow the coordinates, but for some unknown reason, he wanted to go off in the opposite direction. It didn't quite develop into an argument, but it was with great reluctance that he finally agreed to try my way, for a short time, at least. About ten minutes later, he spotted the first massive cairn! I was ecstatic, and to his credit, Bob said, "Thank you for not listening to me!"

All else was forgotten as we hurried to the cairn, and as we approached, we spotted another one, and then another. I resisted the impulse to run around the site like a kid in a candy shop, and instead, stopped to record the coordinates of that first mound of stones and took measurements: N41.15261, W074.17659, and it was approximately 45 feet in diameter. The next mound was even larger, at a whopping 60 feet in diameter, which rang a bell. Having spent a considerable amount of time studying Lenik's 1975 survey map, I knew that the largest stone mound on the site—the 60-footer—was adjacent to three, 45-foot mounds, so I now knew where we stood on the site, in the northeastern quadrant.

I am standing on top of one of the 40-foot-diameter mounds to give an idea of the scale. Until you see them in person, you can't appreciate just how many stones they contain.

Again using Lenik's map, we quickly identified the unusual triple, pointed oval wall/mounds that were aligned due north. The 6-foot boulder on the ridge was plain to see, as was the 15-foot split boulder, both of which were also oriented on a direct north-south line. Two other pairs of mounds and both long and short sections of wall also pointed due north and south. Then there were the numerous walls, some of which were very wide, which just started, stopped and turned for no apparent reason. Wherever you looked, there was stone upon stone, standing as an impressive testament to some group's intensive labors.

The six-foot boulder, above, and 15-foot spilt boulder, below, with Torne Mountain on the horizon.

According to Lenik, whose team partially excavated one of the 45-foot stone mounds which contained "small cobbles," as well as stones weighing hundreds of pounds, all neatly fitted together: "It took six individuals four hours to remove a small section of the stone pile. It was backbreaking work." And for all their effort, they found no artifacts, bones, or other evidence as to the builders or their purpose.

Could there be another type of evidence—clues that can be found in the formations themselves? As there were already six features on the site identified as having a north-south alignment, it was clear that the builders had an awareness of the four cardinal points, and that it had some significance to them—enough of a significance to move tons and tons of rocks. I wondered if there were any other directional indicators, and when a large boulder with prominent white quartz crystals and one flat side caught my eye, I discovered that it was oriented in an east-west direction.

Furthermore, by using the 3D feature on the Garmin, it appeared that if one stood behind that boulder facing east on the spring or fall equinox, the rising sun would come up over the prominent peak of Torne Mountain about 1.25 miles away. While this still requires further study and observation, it was beginning to seem as though there was more than meets the eye here at the Ramapo Walls. Could this be a previously unrecognized calendar site?

While looking at the eight stone mounds in the southwestern quadrant of the site, I was comparing them to the Lenik map and wondered if they had any relation to any constellation or grouping of stars, as the Overlook Mountain site does (see next chapter). As a lifelong amateur astronomer, a cluster like the mounds on the Lenik map reminded me of the Pleiades star cluster, which has had great significance to cultures around the world for thousands of years, including to Native Americans. In Lynn Ceci's article *Watchers of the Pleiades: Ethnoastronomy among Native Cultivators in Northeastern North America*, she states that:

Iroquois and Algonquian cultivators of northeastern North America are among the world's varied cultures to observe the bright cluster of stars known as the Pleiades. According to documentary, ethnographic, and archaeological evidence these northeast natives appear to have related the coincidence of the Pleiades' celestial positions in the spring and fall with the seasonal limits of the frost-free season. This significant discovery, it is proposed, provided a scientific basis for achieving maize productivity in a near-marginal region; it was therefore a critical part of their cultivation technology and as such is reflected in myths and ceremonies.[4]

I was also aware that the Upton Chamber in Massachusetts had a thoroughly researched and documented Pleiades alignment—specifically allowing for the observation of the setting of the stars in the cluster over man-made stone mounds built on top of nearby Pratt Hill. Was something similar going on at the Ramapo Walls? If so, it would be a major discovery.

Photo of the Pleiades star cluster, by Robert Strong.

---

[4] "Watchers of the Pleiades: Ethnoastronomy among Native Cultivators in Northeastern North America," Lynn Ceci, *Ethnohistory,* Vol. 25, No. 4 (Autumn, 1978), pp. 301-317, Duke University Press

I traced the positions of the eight stone mounds on a piece of paper, and then held them against my computer monitor, on which was displayed a photo of the Pleiades star cluster. After adjusting the scale of the photo to match my tracing, I was at first disappointed that there didn't seem to be any correlation, and I could kiss the entire Pleiades/archaeoastronomy idea goodbye. But then I flipped over the tracing and rotated it slightly and let out a bit of a gasp.

Four of the brightest stars in the cluster, which form an irregular box, lined up with the most northerly four of the eight stone mounds! Moving the tracing again, and I found that three more cairns to the south also matched three Pleiades stars! I called to Bob to come and look to see if it was all wishful thinking, but to his surprise, he agreed that it certainly appeared to be a match.

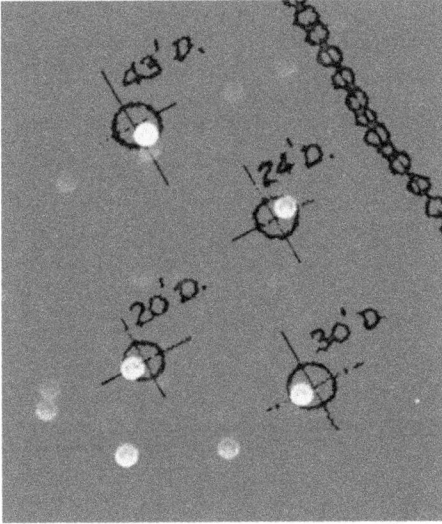

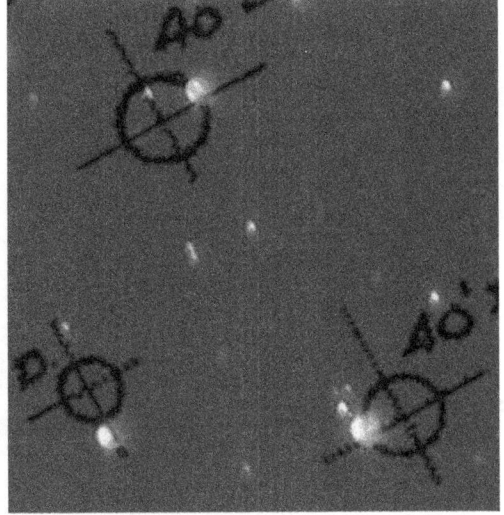

I then grabbed my copy of *Manitou*, in which James Mavor and Byron Dix had scientifically mapped the alignments of the Upton Chamber, and found that the observed direction of the setting of the Pleiades was about 293 degrees. While the Upton site is located in a more northern latitude and the alignment occurred at an elevation of 520 feet over mounds on a hill, the general direction of the setting of the Pleiades at the Ramapo Walls should be in that vicinity. Was there any point of significance on the site where that cluster of stars would set over the four stone mounds?

Excitement rose as I got my 360-degree protractor and placed the center over the stone fireplace indicated on Lenik's map—the only known fireplace on the entire site. The direction of the sightline from that fireplace to the center of those four stone mounds was about 295 degrees, which was certainly in the ballpark for a Pleiades setting. After checking the star positions and movements using the *Stellarium* program online with the coordinates for the site, I confirmed that, depending upon the contour of the horizon along this sightline, the Pleiades would set below view no higher than 299 degrees—just on the southern side of the largest of the four mounds.

However, it got even better, as the positions of the stars change over time. By adjusting the program to the year 1500, the Pleiades set at 296 degrees, which would place it more toward the center of the four mounds. In the year 1000, it set at 293 degrees, almost directly over the center. The point being here, that the Pleiades alignment with these mounds, viewed from a position in line with the fireplace, improves by going back many centuries, certainly adding weight to the argument that this is indeed a very old site.

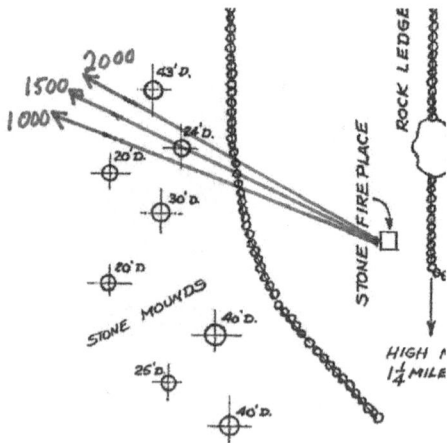

Had I just uncovered the key to this ancient mystery? One arbitrarily chosen location does not a calendar site make, however, so I reached for the equinox/solstice template transparency and placed the center over that fireplace. My jaw dropped as I saw other potential fireplace/mound alignments for winter solstice sunset and summer solstice sunrise! And there were numerous other potential alignments across the site with various features. Could all of this be just a coincidence?

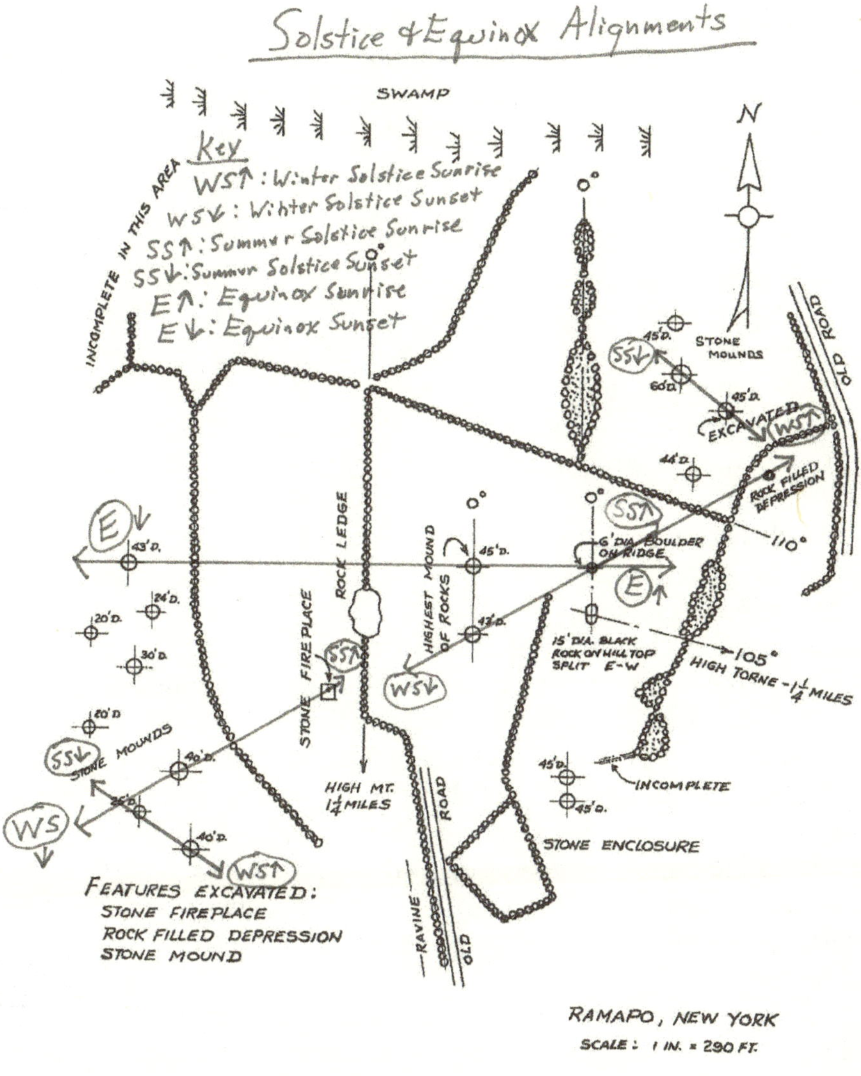

Solstice & Equinox Alignments

Key
WS↑ : Winter Solstice Sunrise
WS↓ : Winter Solstice Sunset
SS↑ : Summer Solstice Sunrise
SS↓ : Summer Solstice Sunset
E↑ : Equinox Sunrise
E↓ : Equinox Sunset

SWAMP

INCOMPLETE IN THIS AREA

STONE MOUNDS

EXCAVATED

ROCK FILLED DEPRESSION

110°

ROCK LEDGE

6' DIA. BOULDER ON RIDGE

15' DIA. BLACK ROCK ON HILLTOP SPLIT E-W

HIGHEST MOUND OF ROCKS

STONE FIRE PLACE

HIGH MT. 1¼ MILES

105°
HIGH TORNE - 1¼ MILES

INCOMPLETE

STONE MOUNDS

STONE ENCLOSURE

RAVINE

OLD ROAD

OLD ROAD

FEATURES EXCAVATED:
STONE FIREPLACE
ROCK FILLED DEPRESSION
STONE MOUND

RAMAPO, NEW YORK
SCALE: 1 IN. = 290 FT.

I had to temper my enthusiasm, as just the map alone was deceiving in a way, because it didn't depict the rolling terrain and changes in elevation. It was also spread out over 200 acres. In other words, these alignments looked good on paper, but would you actually be able to *see* a specific mound or boulder from a potential alignment viewing location?

During an even more extensive study of the site on another hike, which happened to occur on New Year's Day of 2016, I quickly dismissed the possibility of most of the features on the western edge of the site being visible on the eastern side, as the north/south wall roughly in the center of the site is positioned along a ridge that drops off to the west, eliminating a direct line of sight. But what about features that were closer together?

One of the main points of interest to Lenik and his team was the "stone filled depression" on the eastern edge of the site. His description of the feature is as follows:

"As the excavation of the depression was completed, it was found to be rectangular in shape, measuring 4 ft. long by 2 ft., 3 in. wide. It was not very deep, going down to a maximum of 2 ft., 2 in. below the present ground level and terminating in bedrock. The depression appeared to be man-made as many of the stones seemed to be definitely placed in position to give the hole its rectangular shape...Our original questions remain; who built it and why? A great deal of work went into placing these stones in the depression."

If such care had been taken by the builders, might there be special significance to this spot? By using the survey map and my solstice/equinox template, it looked as though anyone standing in that depression would be able to observe the all-important winter solstice sunset over the 6-foot boulder so prominently positioned on the ridge, about 500 feet away. But was there a direct line of site?

It could be difficult to tell with all of the trees that now cover the site, but we had to try. While Bob stood at the depression, I walked over to the 6-foot boulder. Fortunately, I was wearing my bright yellow jacket, and over the walkie-talkie, Bob kept me informed that I was "still in sight." I did go out of view for a few steps here or there due to the trees, but the real test came when I climbed atop the boulder and anxiously asked if he could see me.

"As clear as day!" he replied, much to my delight.

There is no doubt, then, that cleared of trees, anyone standing in the stone-filled depression on the evening of the winter solstice could watch the setting sun dip behind this boulder on the ridge! This was definitely a calendar site!

Of all the stone sites that I have explored, I feel that the Ramapo Walls are the most intriguing. I'm sure I have only scratched the surface of this incredible site, and hope to return for many years to come to observe solar, lunar, and stellar alignments.

Of course, as always, the question remains as to who built the walls and mounds, and when? Hopefully, archaeoastronomy will help date when the site began. As to who the builders were, in my opinion, we once again need look no further than the countless generations of people who called this area home for thousands of years.

Possible lunar cycle alignments.

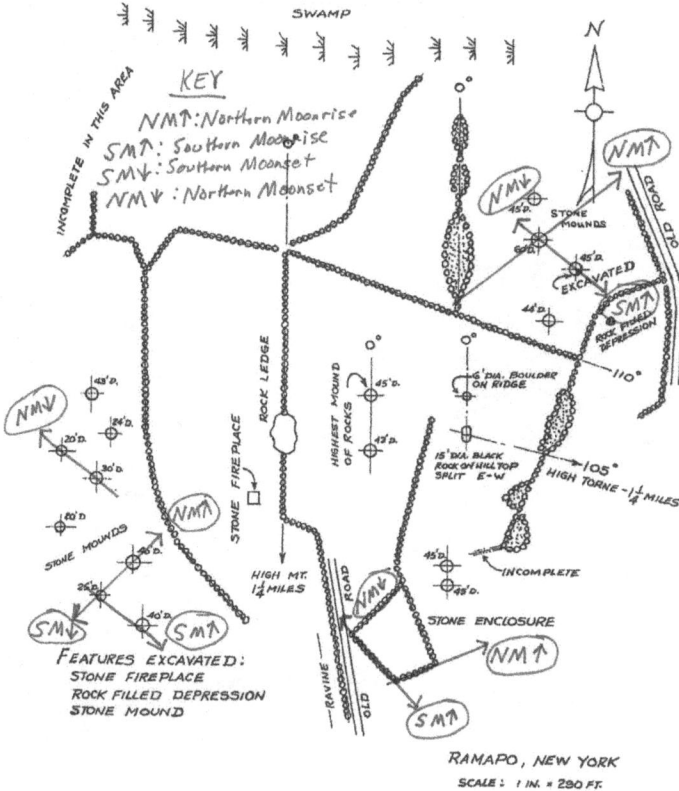

RAMAPO, NEW YORK
SCALE : 1 IN. = 280 FT.

New Discoveries at Ramapo Walls Site

Please go to page 169 for some startling new material about this site.

Lifting Rocks
Deerpark, New York

Route 97 through the Hawk's Nest in the town of Deerpark, NY is one of the most scenic drives in the region with its steep cliffs towering over the Delaware River below. If someone wanted to have a prominent signaling location using bonfires, they could be seen for miles from the top of this mountain. And if someone wanted to construct a calendar or ceremonial site in this area, this would also be an ideal location.

There is such a site called Lifting Rocks, and it may have first been mentioned in the 1890s in a book by James Allerton, *The Hawks Nest, or the Last of the Cahoonshees: A Tale of the Delaware Valley and*

Historical Romance of 1690. If this is the same site Allerton saw, then he appears to have used considerable poetic license in his exaggerated description of boulders "weighing from 30 to 100 tons, elevated above the ground 5 feet and resting on three stone pillars. These pillars are equal distance apart –as much so as if they had been placed there on geometrical principles."

The reality is a far more modest collection of boulders on support stones, but the smaller size in no way detracts from the possible significance of the site. There is one boulder which is triangular in shape, and it points to High Point in New Jersey, just ten miles away. It is the highest mountain in New Jersey, and there were reports that another stone site once stood at its summit—until it was destroyed in the construction of the massive war memorial built in 1930. However, High Point has other stone sites nearby which are described in the following section.

Of astronomical significance, is a line of two boulders and a roughly circular, shallow pit. Salvatore Trento suggested that an observer sitting in this pit could view the Major Lunar Standstill along the line of the two boulders. As this lunar event occurs only once every 18.61 years, this would necessitate an excellent knowledge of astronomy, and a long period of habitation or use at this site to pinpoint the alignment.

The property which contains Lifting Rocks is now privately owned by a hunting club, but Mike knew one of the members and was able to arrange for us to visit. It is a fascinating site with many features, and we spent a considerable amount of time taking measurements and exploring as best we could through all the thick vegetation. (And much to our dismay, and disgust, we later discovered that we had each amassed a large collection of ticks in the process!)

Using Trento's sketch of the site, I decided to follow the line of the purported lunar alignment farther out. I knew that white quartz was often present in ancient stone sites to mark something of importance, and it was also used to represent the Moon, so I played a hunch and started walking. Mike and our guide stood on top of the two boulders so I could use them as a sightline, and with a compass I went through the often waist-high weeds (collecting even more ticks, no doubt) until I came upon a marvelous site—a huge, domed, chunk of white quartz!

I searched all over the area and couldn't find a likely source for the quartz, so it appeared as though it was deliberately transported to the site and placed there on purpose. And what better purpose for a bright, white piece of quartz than to represent an important lunar alignment?

Another curiosity which caught my eye was an oval boulder that had holes on one side. They did not appear to be the result of simple weathering, but looked like man-made chisel or drill marks. Since we were measuring everything else, I decided to determine the distance between these holes and found a remarkable thing–there appeared to be a pattern in the measurements of 6 inches, 12 inches, 18 inches, and 30 inches. These numbers are part of a Fibonacci Sequence, where subsequent numbers are the sum of the previous two numbers. Either this was an incredible coincidence, or someone with an excellent knowledge of mathematics had made these holes.

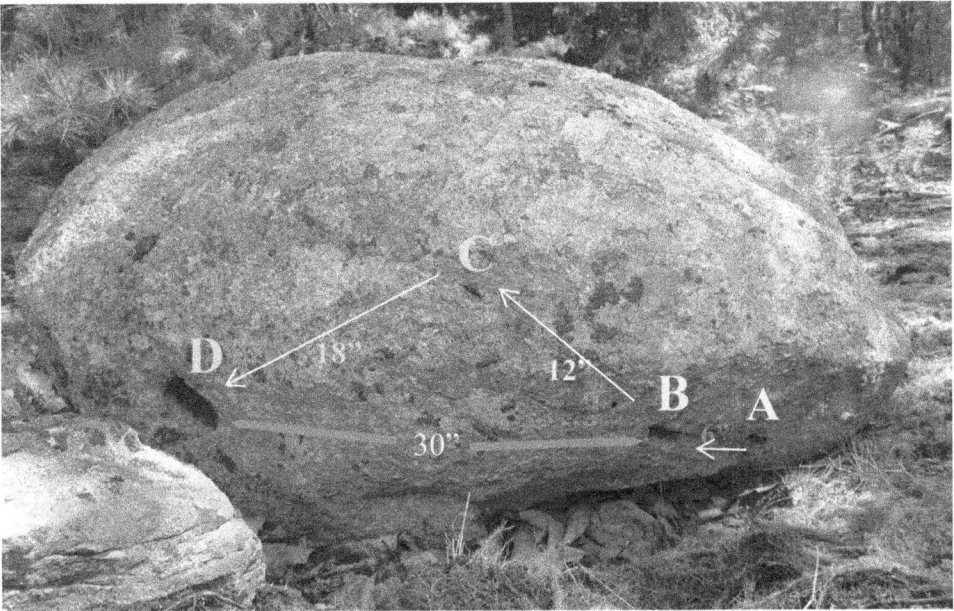

Mike and I also found numerous examples of lines in the stones, but couldn't tell whether or not they were the results of natural fracturing and weathering, or were man-made.

In any event, Lifting Rocks is a site that deserves study by archaeologists, astronomers, and geologists, to fully determine the extent of any alignments and other possible features.

Lifting Rocks is located on private property and is not available to the public. The property is owned by an active hunting club, so it is both illegal and dangerous to trespass.

High Point
High Point State Park, Sussex, New Jersey

The story of the discovery of the High Point State Park calendar site is a testament to the power of curiosity and the value of exploration and observation. Countless people over the years had passed by three huge boulders in the park—in fact, one had been propped up to secure it, and the other had an official plaque attached to it—but no one realized their significance until 1976, and only then it was as the result of looking for something else.

High Point is aptly named, as it is the highest point in the state of New Jersey, at 1,803 feet at the top of a peak in the Kittatinny Mountains. It is now capped by a towering, 220-foot war memorial obelisk commissioned by Colonel Anthony Kuser, completed in 1930, which can be seen for many miles. Kuser had also built a mansion on the mountain, and later donated the land to the state of New Jersey, who turned it into a state park. While the obelisk is an impressive site, it may have replaced a much older, possibly ancient stone site that is rumored to have been there. True or not, fortunately not all of the stone features in the area were destroyed or moved.

In Thomas Brannan's article, *Calendar Sites at High Point, New Jersey*, published in *North Jersey Highlander*[5] in 1980, he describes how

---

[5] *Calendar Site at High Point, New Jersey*, Thomas F. Brannan, *North Jersey Highlander*, North Jersey Highlands Historical Society, Summer, 1980, pages 27-31.

he and a friend, Ralph "Robby" Robinson, were investigating a "series of mountaintop fireplaces" in the region, which they believed formed a "silent signal system." They did indeed find a possible signal fireplace at High Point, but while mapping the area, they also noticed two rows of boulders that formed what appeared to be winter and summer solstice sunrise alignments. While the summer solstice alignment was confirmed by observation, the winter solstice alignment appeared to be slightly off. However, a single boulder to the right of the row did mark the exact winter solstice sunrise, as if someone was trying to refine the alignment but never got around to moving the other boulders.

Intrigued, and looking for more possible alignments, Robinson scouted the site from an airplane and noticed three huge boulders along the west side of Lake Marcia. Excited by the find, he and Brannan expected that by standing behind these boulders, they would be able to watch the solstice and equinox sunrises occur over the High Point peak. According to Brannan, "This seemed to be a good idea, but it turned out to be wrong. Like many wrong ideas, however, it generated the right idea."

Equinox boulder and the notch between the mountains.

At dawn of the spring equinox of 1978, the two men stood behind the suspected equinox boulder and anxiously awaited a dramatic sunrise over the top of High Point. It didn't happen. What did occur was the sun rising directly in the center of the notch between High Point and the adjacent peak. By standing about ten feet behind the boulder, the alignment matched up beautifully. Subsequent observations for the summer and winter solstice sunrises confirmed that by standing about ten feet behind the corresponding boulders, the sun also rose up out of that notch!

The point of the summer solstice boulder and the notch.

In addition, they later found a boulder which was in the perfect spot to be illuminated at sunrise on the first day of May. This, along with the two calendar sites, made it obvious that these were not chance alignments of boulders simply dropped by glaciers. They may indeed have been dropped by glaciers in the area, but it was the hand of man who moved them to their important positions.

Winter solstice sunrise boulder.

On a hot, sunny, late summer day in 2013, Mike and I went to see this site for ourselves and identify the three boulders. They were not hard to find, as the first two—for summer solstice and the equinoxes—are right along the west side of the road that runs beside the lake. It was nice to finally have a site that was easy to locate, but it also gave me pause to think how close they came to being moved during construction of the road or parking lots. The third boulder, for winter solstice, is in front of the Activity Center, and could also have easily been demolished when the center was being built.

We took a lot of photos and verified the compass directions from the three boulders to the notch in the mountains. But that was not the end of our mission. There was also supposed to be a large perched boulder off a trail somewhere to the south. After unsuccessfully trying a couple of possible trails—which was no small exertion in the intense heat—we stopped by the Visitor's Center for help.

We were very surprised to find that the park personnel had only just recently heard about the calendar stones—which should be the main features on their park maps!—but they did know what we were talking about regarding the perched boulder, or Tripod Rock as it was also known.

It was off the Rutherford Trail, about half a mile south of the Visitor's Center. That was about the extent of our directions, but at least we now knew the correct trail.

The heat and humidity that day were the kind that slaps you in the face like a hot, wet towel when you open the door of your air-conditioned car. Mike and I had already been on our feet hiking uphill and down for hours, but we were both determined to find the Tripod Rock. Of course, as luck would have it, the trail branched off at several points, one of which led past crumbling hills of black shale. Let me tell you, the sun beating down on that black rock and radiating up like a blast furnace started to melt our resolve, but we hung in there and kept searching.

Finally, we found a metal gate that had paths leading to both the left and right. I went right into the tall weeds, and Mike went left, up a rocky slope. A couple of minutes later I heard the faint, but beautiful shout of victory that Mike had found the Tripod Rock. I hurried toward the sound of his voice and stopped short when the impressive, 10-foot-long rock came into view beneath a low, rocky ridge. This was one cool, triangular perched boulder, with its supports deliberately placed in the three corners, pointing like a massive road sign to something, but to what?

In fact, the point of Tripod Rock aims directly west. Whether or not it was just a directional marker, or it was pointing to an important location to the west has yet to be determined—and may never be determined—but some group obviously went to a great effort to move and position this triangular rock on its triangular base. Geologists have said that while the rock is from a local source, it was a glacier that dropped it on this site, but even they have to admit the hand of man placed the support stones beneath it. What no one had mentioned previously, however, was that it had been positioned due west, which gives it even more significance.

It was a very successful and exciting day, but with heat exhaustion looming and hunger setting in, we called it a day at that point, but I knew I would eventually return.

Even though the alignments of the High Point calendar site have been well documented and observed on numerous occasions, I naturally wanted to see one for myself. On the chilly, windy morning of the fall equinox in 2013, Bob and I walked through the darkness to the Equinox Boulder and awaited the approaching dawn. The sky was clear and the moon was bright, and I had cameras and camcorders at the ready. As the minutes ticked by, however, shivering in the cold, I couldn't believe my eyes as a thin layer of clouds began to form just along the eastern horizon—and nowhere else.

"No! Not again!" I moaned, as this would be the umpteenth time the weather had thwarted an attempt to view a solstice or equinox sunrise or sunset.

We held out hope that there might be a break in the clouds, or that they would dissipate in time, but no such luck. However, even though there was that band of clouds, the rising sun did create a very bright spot in the center of the notch which confirmed that this was indeed an equinox calendar stone. At that moment, I got a chill of another kind—how many generations of people in the distant past stood on this spot and watched this site on equinox morning? And who were those people?

Theories range from Native Americans to pre-Columbian Europeans, possibly Celts or pagans who celebrated May Day. I once again gravitate toward the Native Americans. Their lives depended upon knowing when the seasons would change, so it is only natural that they created a lasting way to mark important days in the calendar, and what better way than with stone and mountains?

The precariously perched support stones in the front of Tripod Rock.

Directions to the Park Entrance: Take Route 23 approximately 7 miles north of the town of Sussex, NJ, or 4 miles south of Port Jervis, NY. Please see their website for the current list of fees and hours: www.njparksandforests.com/parks/highpoint.html

Summer Solstice Rock: N41.31599, W074.66892
Equinox Rock: N41.31829, W074.66832
Winter Solstice Rock: N41.32029, W074.66745

To Tripod Rock: Head south from High Point State Park on Route 23. You will pass the Appalachian Trail parking lot, and 0.4 miles south of that will be a turnoff with a yellow metal gate at coordinates N41.300334, W074.663024. Take the trail beyond the gate until you come to a smaller gate, where you will make an immediate left just past that gate. The Tripod Rock is just steps away, at coordinates: N41.29491, W074.66365

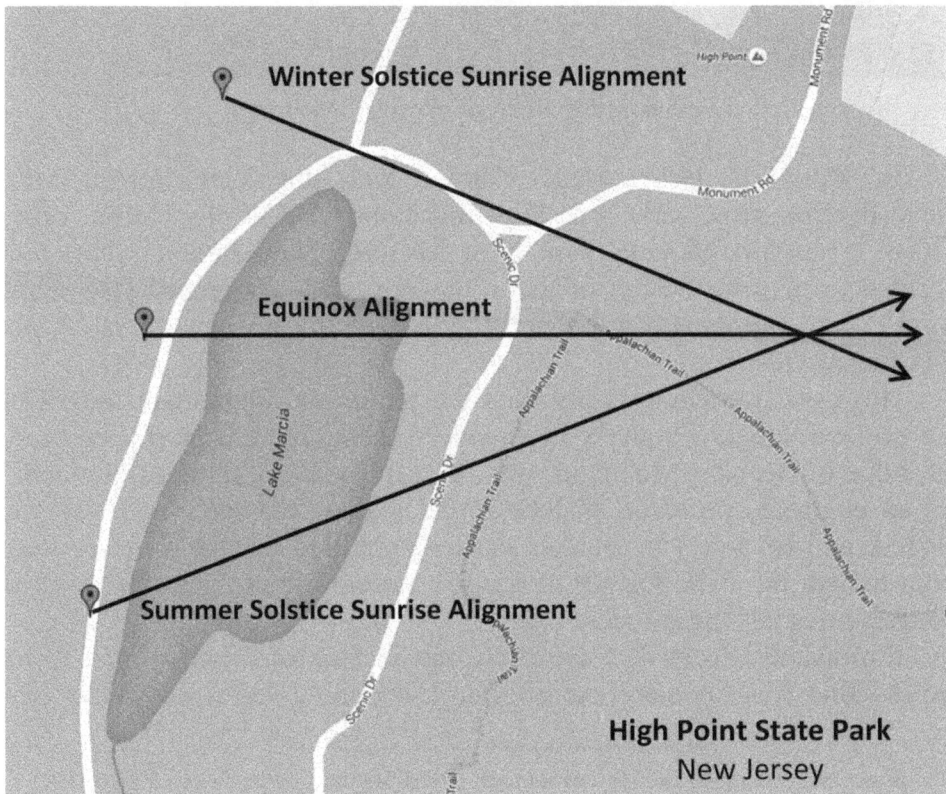

Winter Solstice Sunrise Alignment

Equinox Alignment

Lake Marcia

Summer Solstice Sunrise Alignment

High Point State Park
New Jersey

Bearfort Mountain
West Milford, New Jersey

West Pointing Rock on Bearfort Mountain

In April of 1980, Mead Stapler and Jim Van Hooker were "investigating some early lime kilns and family burial plots in the valley below"[6] Bearfort Mountain in West Milford, New Jersey, when they decided to hike to the top of the 1300-foot peak. As if the steep climb wasn't enough, they also went up the tall fire tower to "enjoy the spectacular view."

However, something other than the picturesque mountain ranges on the horizon caught Stapler's eye—below them, running northeast along the ridge of Bearfort Mountain, was "a suspicious grouping of boulders." As an engineer, surveyor, historian, and author, Stapler's curiosity was piqued, and he and Van Hooker were determined to take a closer look, even though the Park Ranger in the fire tower warned them that a lot of "snakes infested" those rocks.

Fortunately, no snakes appeared, but in Stapler's own words, "what we did find was far more exciting, an astonishing series of perched and

---

[6] *Stone Alignments on Bearfort Mountain*, Mead Stapler, *North Jersey Highlander*, Winter 1980, 23-26

aligned boulders stretching along the spine of the mountain for about 1500 feet." They realized that this site could be of great importance, so they returned in six weeks with two additional members of the North Jersey Highlands Historical Society and conducted a detailed survey of the site.

The results were remarkable, with "at least ten intentionally perched boulders," which the team believed were perched to denote some special significance. In addition, there were stones arranged in an equilateral triangle, and not one, but two trios of stones placed equidistant and in straight lines, one of which was in a north-south alignment.

One of the lines of boulders.

In all, the team mapped and measured 29 boulders that appeared to have been deliberately positioned by the hand of man. Many of the stones were composed of Green Pond Conglomerate, a local puddingstone, so named as its small, often colorful, imbedded pebbles resembles the dried fruits in a Christmas pudding. However, there was a single, bizarre, blackish limestone boulder noted, as it was unlike anything else at the site.

The perched and aligned stones of Bearfort Mountain were all a great mystery, and in puzzling over their origins, Stapler commented:

"Presently, the theory of the purpose of these sites fall into one of two categories, either that of having some astronomical significance or being part of a system of cross country trail guides. The archaeological 'establishment' of course either ignores the subject completely or passes it off as the work of nature or mentally unbalanced colonials."

While I had to laugh at Stapler's comment about such stone sites being considered to be nothing more than the work of "mentally unbalanced colonials," he was unfortunately correct about archaeologists ignoring Bearfort Mountain. Other than a few brief references in hiking guides about interesting rocks along the top of the ridge, in the 36 years since Stapler and his team published their findings, an Internet search was unable to turn up any additional research conducted at this site. This didn't really surprise me, but it was certainly disappointing.

The blackish limestone rock. The trail is below.

Just by examining the site survey, it was evident that there were at least six possible solstice and equinox sunrise/sunset alignments. And upon visiting the site, it became evident that the sightlines for these possible alignments would be unimpeded if the ridge was cleared of trees. In fact, if this ridge was clear, the profusion of boulders would be nothing short of stunning. Even with the trees, the sight of these large stones dotting the landscape in every direction you looked was very impressive.

114

Bearfort Mountain

Linda Zimmermann 2016
Based on GPS coordinates
obtained with Garmin Oregon 450s

N ↑

Equinox Alignment

270° — P.B. — 90°

SS↑ ↓ WS↓ P.B.
alignment

Perched Boulders

West Pointing Rock

Key

SS↑ - Summer Solstice Sunrise
SS↓ - Summer Solstice Sunset
WS↑ - Winter Solstice Sunrise
WS↓ - Winter Solstice Sunset
P.B. - Perched Boulder

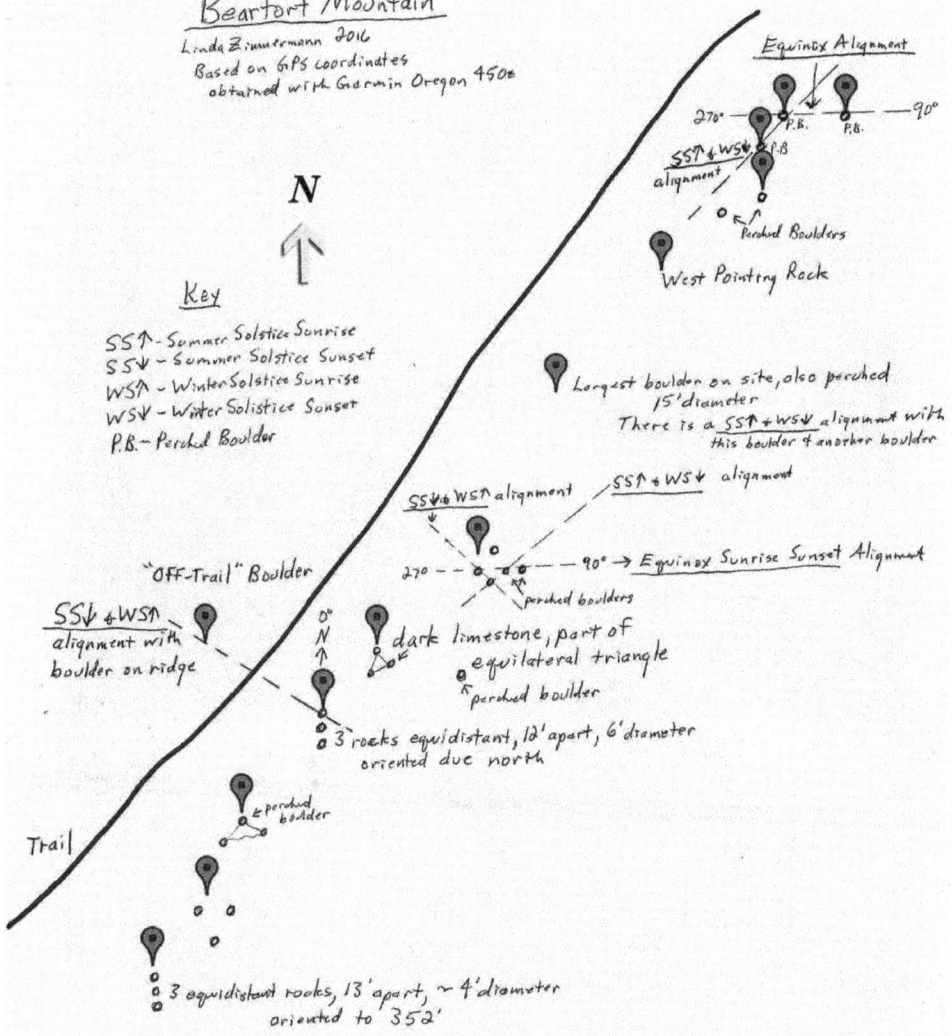

Largest boulder on site, also perched
15' diameter
There is a SS↑ ↓ WS↓ alignment with
this boulder & another boulder

SS↓ ↓ WS↑ alignment   SS↑ ↓ WS↓ alignment

270 — o oo — 90° → Equinox Sunrise Sunset Alignment

perched boulders

"Off-Trail" Boulder

SS↓ ↓ WS↑
alignment with
boulder on ridge

0°
N
↑

dark limestone, part of
equilateral triangle
↑ perched boulder

3 rocks equidistant, 12' apart, 6' diameter
oriented due north

Trail

& perched
boulder

3 equidistant rocks, 13' apart, ~ 4' diameter
oriented to 352'

Speaking of looking in all directions, about midway down the ridge, Bob noticed a very large boulder below and to the west, on the other side of the trail. I took some photos and made a mental note to examine it once I was finished obtaining coordinates and photos on top of the ridge, which took quite a while. I took coordinates from the main features on Stapler's

115

survey map, but in retrospect, I wish I had plotted every large stone along the ridge. However, very cold winds, along with this being the second long hike in as many days, was sapping my energy, so I contented myself that the data I did collect was sufficient for this initial visit.

The two sides of largest boulder on the site.

We descended the steep ridge at a safe location to examine what I termed the "off trail" boulder. I took photographs of the large chunk of puddingstone, recorded its coordinates, then turned around and noticed we were beneath a boulder on the ridge. I got that sneaking suspicion that this prominent and obvious positioning was not a mere coincidence, so I took a compass reading from the off-trail boulder and the boulder on the ridge and found that it was 120 degrees—the heading of winter solstice sunrise!

However, given the elevation differences, I think the better observing point would be on the ridge looking down, where summer solstice sunset should be directly over that off-trail boulder! Just a short distance away, there was another off-trail boulder which also had a corresponding boulder up on the ridge. And guess what, this pair of boulders also had a winter solstice sunrise/summer solstice sunset alignment! What were the chances?

One of the boulders on the ridge as seen from an off-trail boulder.

Of course, as always, the best way to confirm these alignments is with direct observation, but I would suggest an entire team of observers, as there are so many stones on Bearfort Mountain to consider. What other secrets are there to unlock at this incredible site? In addition to solar and lunar alignments, are there also constellation and star alignments? Let's hope another 36 years doesn't pass before we find out...

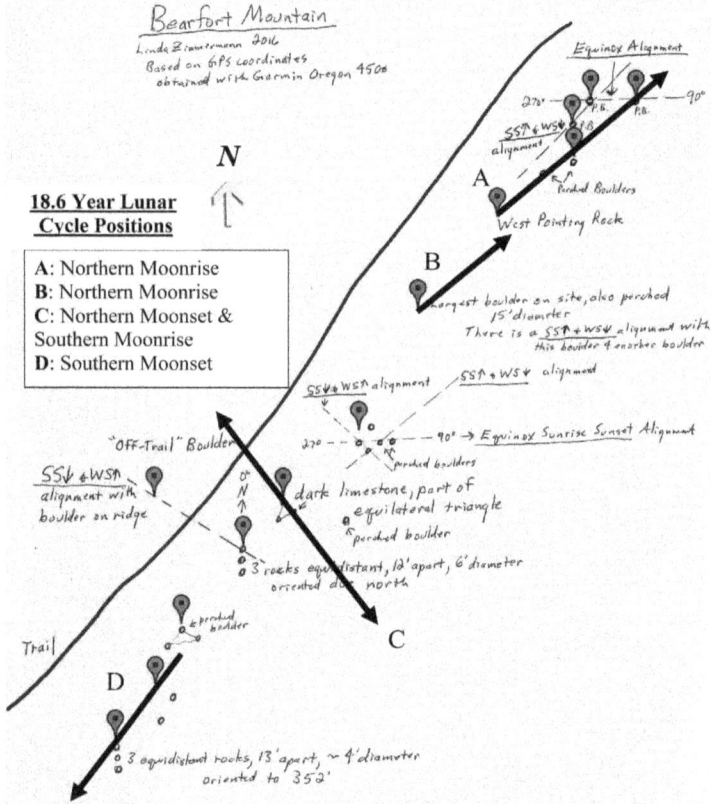

Possible lunar alignments between boulders on Bearfort Mountain.

Directions: Permits for Bearfort Mtn. must be obtained in person in Newfoundland, New Jersey at 223 Echo Lake Road. Trail parking is at the end of Stephens Road, West Milford. Trail maps are available online. GPS coordinates for the north end boulder are: N41.10775, W074.41356

Tripod Rock
Kinnelon, NJ

It was a frigid thirteen degrees with an unspeakable wind chill factor the December 2013 morning that Bob and I arrived at Pyramid Mountain in Kinnelon, New Jersey—and it only got worse the higher we climbed. However, despite the painfully cold weather and the steepness of the trail, it was all worth it the moment the massive Tripod Rock came into view.

This may be the largest of all the perched boulders in the Northeast, weighing in at an estimated 130 tons, and measuring about 18 feet long and 10 feet wide, with a perched height of 8 feet. There is also an unusual triangular crest which runs along the top surface. The stone is composed of gneiss of relatively local origin, and probably did not travel more than

20 miles with the Wisconsin Glacier that deposited it on Pyramid Mountain.

The crest on top of Tripod Rock.

Tripod Rock is so named because it has three supporting stones, which form an approximate 3-4-5 triangle. One tripod rock on a mountain is curious enough, but this site has numerous tripod rocks and perched boulders, seriously diminishing the probability that they are all natural. Add to that, the fact that two smaller tripod rocks and a group of stones have a summer solstice sunset alignment, and that probability drops even lower.

In a *Skylands Visitor* online article, even the assistant naturalist for Pyramid Mountain, Allison Para, admits that some of the boulders were most likely moved by the hand of man.

"We believe the Solstice Stones were placed there (by Native Americans) because it was probably a ceremonial site. The sun sets between those two rocks," Para stated.

This may appear to be a simple statement, but it is actually huge in the realm of the stone sites controversy, as it is an official admission that Native Americans in this area aligned stones and made calendar sites. For researchers such as me, who have repeatedly heard the mantra of "Native

Americans in the Northeast didn't build anything in stone," this is a breath of fresh air. Granted, perched boulders are not structures, per se, but they do require extensive knowledge of the movement of the sun, and considerable planning and cooperation in transporting and accurately placing these large stones.

Summer solstice sunset occurs between these two boulders.

This solstice alignment, however, was once even more complex, as there used to be another boulder on an adjacent ridge to the west of this site. In the past, you would not only look between the two Solstice Stones, but out across a half-mile valley to this distant boulder to line up the setting sun on the evening of the summer solstice—like the bead sight on the end of a rifle. Unfortunately, I say "in the past," because a house was built on that ridge in the early 1980s, and during construction that boulder was thoughtlessly dislodged and moved—thus destroying an alignment that could have been in place for thousands of years.

A partial site survey sketch by Bruce Scofield appeared in the Summer/Fall 1983 NEARA Journal article "A Possible Summer Solstice Marker in Northern New Jersey." No other alignments were identified in this article, but when I superimposed my solstice/equinox template over the sketch, I found something interesting. If one were to stand on a theoretical Observation Point X, then summer solstice sunrise would occur over Rock M, winter solstice sunrise would occur over Rock N, and winter solstice sunset would occur over the Tripod Rock. While this is all speculation based on the survey sketch, here we have not one, not two, but three very important alignments which could be observed from a single spot! Of course, these would all need to be confirmed by observations made on the solstices.

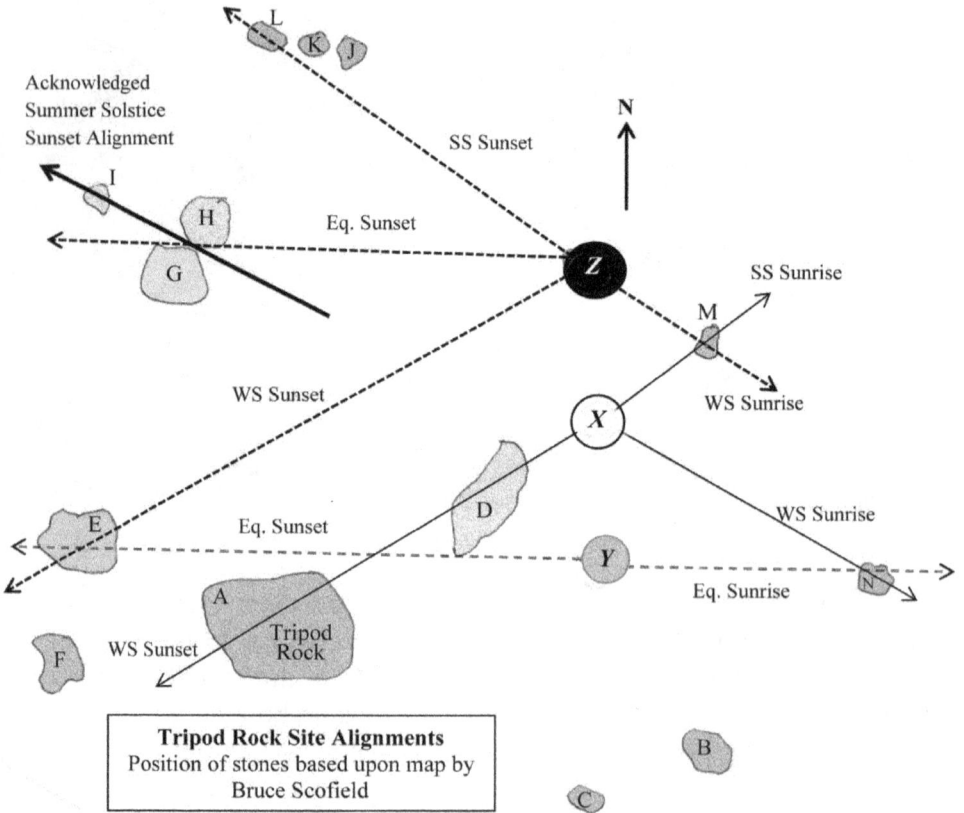

Tripod Rock Site Alignments
Position of stones based upon map by
Bruce Scofield

Literally taking a few steps backward to Observation Point Y would create an equinox sunrise and sunset alignment from Rock N, grazing the point of the Bedrock Outcrop D, and over the center of Rock E. Or, if one were sitting on top of the Tripod Rock, equinox sunset would occur between Rock E and Rock F.

A few steps forward to Observation Point Z would also allow for multiple alignments: winter solstice sunrise over Rock M, summer solstice sunset over Rock L, equinox sunset through Rocks G and H, and winter solstice sunset over Rock E. And with more rocks and perched boulders around the site not contained in the survey, there may be many more solar and lunar alignments.

I must repeat the disclaimer that given any set of rocks you can find alignments, but when these proposed observation points yield two, three, and four major alignments standing on the same spot, it seems to go beyond coincidence. It would also make sense that if the Native Americans did indeed move and perch the Summer Solstice Stones into position and believed this site had some significance, they would have utilized the other rocks on the site to mark additional important dates and astronomical events. And perhaps these multiple alignment spots indicate that, like the Lake Tiorati Calendar Site, it was constructed and refined in different phases over the course of many years.

All of these theoretical alignments I have proposed here need to be confirmed by actual observations, but even if they all prove to be inaccurate, this is a very important site in that it has been recognized as a Native American calendar site to mark the summer solstice sunset. And what other archaeoastronomical features are yet to be found in the surrounding landscape? Lace up your hiking boots and see what you can discover!

For directions and more information:
www.nynjtc.org/park/pyramid-mountain
When we visited, trail maps were available at the parking lot.
Coordinates of the Tripod Rock: N40.96110, W074.38519

The Curious Case of 353
(Or is it 173?)

While taking measurements at the Indian Hill site, I noticed that two of the massive walls were pointing toward 353 degrees. I think I was hoping that they were oriented due north and south, so I checked and rechecked, but confirmed that it was indeed 353 degrees in one direction, or 173 degrees in the opposite direction. If it had only been one wall, I probably wouldn't have given it much more thought, but two massive walls with the same orientation was not random, so the numbers stuck in my head.

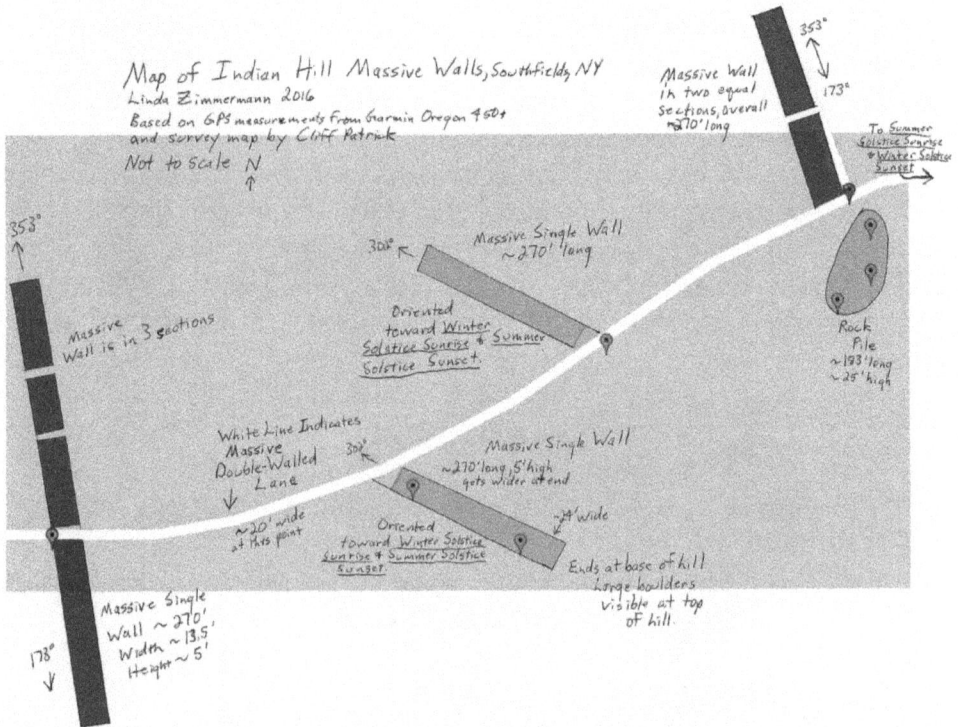

The black-shaded walls at each end are oriented to 353/173 degrees.

Then, as I was writing the Bearfort Mountain story, I noticed on the bottom of Mead Stapler's map that he had found three boulders in a line which he indicated were oriented to 352 degrees, just a 1 degree difference, which wasn't much, considering in 1980 he was using a conventional compass and then correcting for magnetic declination. Unfortunately, I did not personally measure the heading of this line of boulders, as at the time, I didn't know other sites had a similar alignment.

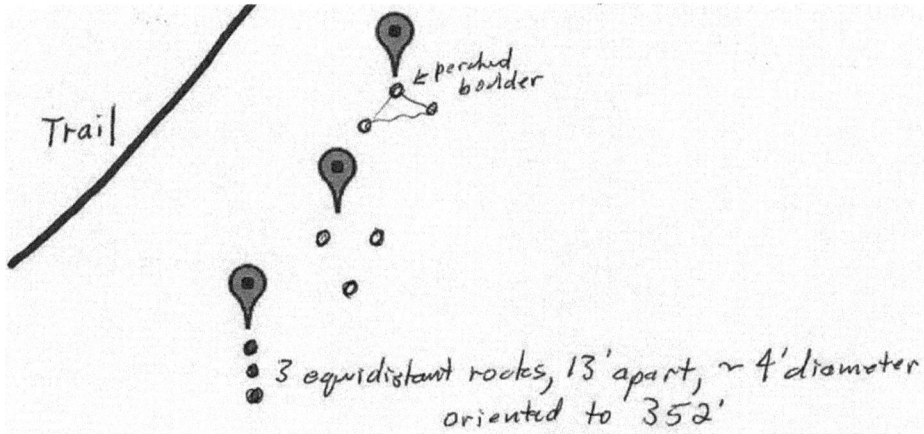

Bearfort Mountain line of boulders with a 352 degree alignment, at the south end of the site.

That got the wheels turning. Were there other 353/173 alignments at any of the other sites? To my astonishment, there were! There were such alignments at both Lake Tiorati and the Ramapo Walls! That made four different sites, two of which had multiple 353/173 alignments. One of the walls at the King's Chamber site may also be oriented to 353/173. What were the chances?

Taking a stab in the dark, I did an Internet search for "353 173 degrees alignment," and actually got a hit. And my jaw dropped when I opened the reference and found that this alignment was in that most ancient stone site of Gobekli Tepe in Turkey! In the largest enclosure excavated so far, the two huge central monoliths were both oriented to 353/173. And another pair of central monoliths in a different enclosure was just a few degrees off at 350 and 170. What was going on?

Now let me state right off the bat that I don't think there is *any* connection between the people who built Gobekli Tepe 11,000 years ago and the builders of the calendar sites in the Hudson Valley. What I will suggest, however, is that there may be some significant celestial object that either rises or sets at either 353 or 173 degrees. Although given the fact that star positions move over time due to precession, I can't imagine that the builders of Gobekli Tepe were seeing the same star positions as were seen in the Hudson Valley in the last millennia.

The ancient site of Gobekli Tepe in Turkey.

An illustration of precession: As the earth wobbles like a spinning top, the positions of the stars change over the course of 26,000 years.

So, concentrating just on the Hudson Valley sites, I spent a considerable amount of time with the Stellarium program checking the risings and settings of stars at 353/173 degrees for all months of the year and many different years going back centuries, but was unable to find anything of obvious significance. Of course, we can't ever know exactly what was important to ancient people. Was there a transient event like a comet or supernova? Did some obscure star have special meaning to these people?

I personally find it difficult to believe that seven examples of the 353/173 alignments at five different calendar sites in the area is simply a case of random positioning and coincidence. But unfortunately, why the builders chose this specific alignment remains a mystery...for now.

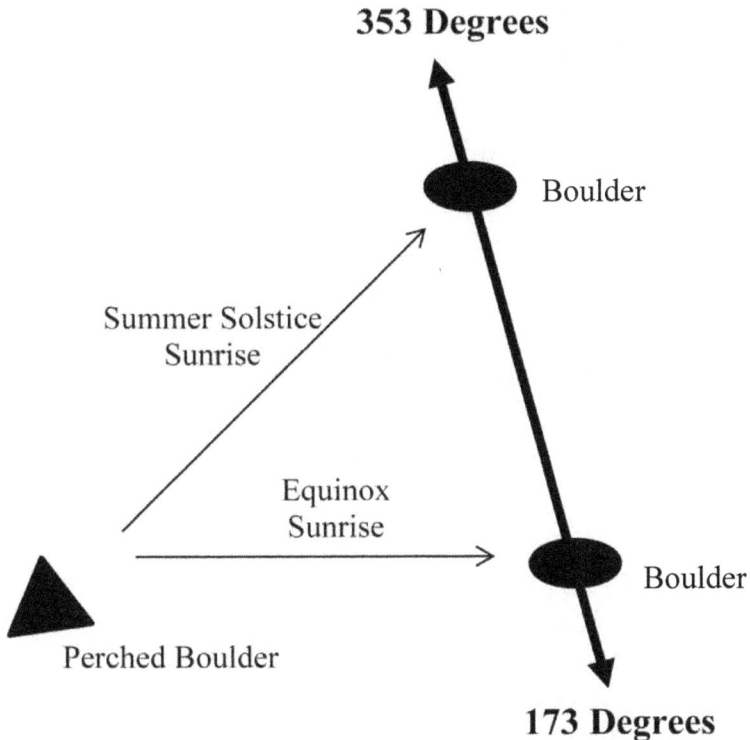

353 Degrees

Boulder

Summer Solstice
Sunrise

Equinox
Sunrise

Boulder

Perched Boulder

173 Degrees

The Lake Tiorati 353/173 degree alignment.

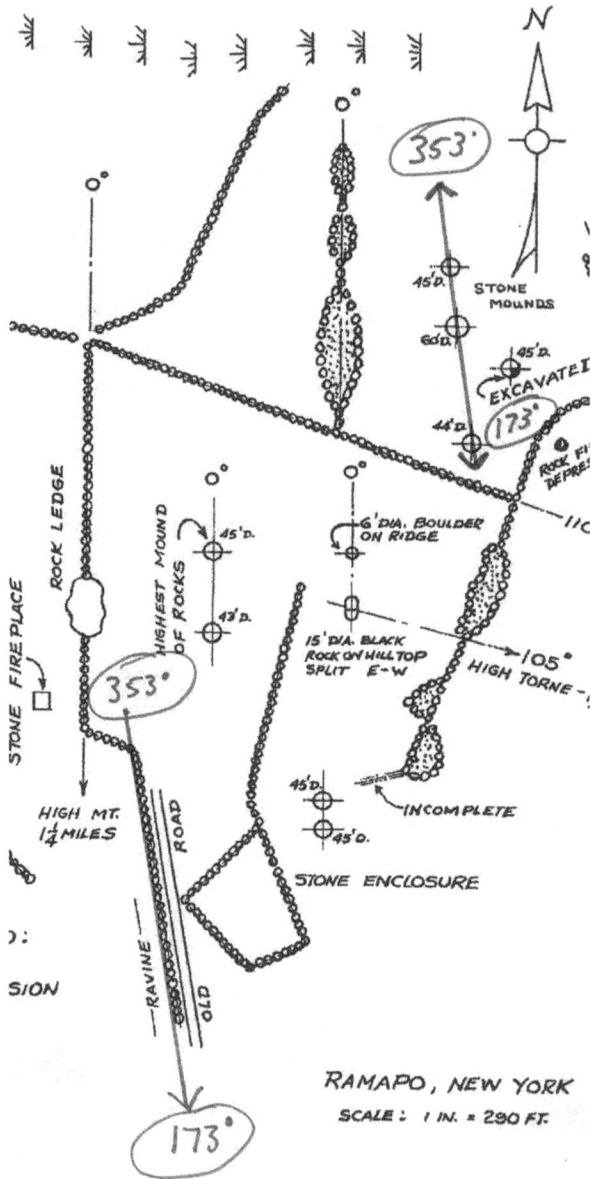

Ramapo Walls: A line of three cairns, including the largest on the site, and an approximately 635-foot section of wall have the 353/173 degree alignment.

More Mysteries

The following is a fascinating collection of cairns, effigies, standing stones, and other unique features in the Hudson Valley.

Overlook Mountain Center
Woodstock, New York

One of the carefully constructed cairns.

The Overlook Mountain Center in Woodstock, New York, is a non-profit organization formed in 2013 dedicated to the preservation of an amazing landscape of stone cairns and walls, which had been threatened by development. Chairperson Glenn Kreisberg, who is also an author and former Vice President of NEARA, spearheaded the campaign to raise funding to purchase the land, and create educational programs to bring awareness and appreciation to this unique site.

Michael Worden and I were fortunate to get a tour from Glenn of the fascinating grouping of neatly stacked stone cairns and serpent walls which undulate up the mountain slopes. While to the average hiker these cairns may all look like random piles of stones, Glenn made an important observation—several of the cairns are placed in the same positions as the stars in the constellation Draco, which looks like a snake in the sky. This discovery adds critical evidence to the fact that this was a sacred landscape that deserves our respect and understanding.

One of the undulating "bodies" of the snake which goes up a steep hill, and ends at the massive "head."

OMC should be an example to other communities to study and preserve similar sites. The more we understand our past, the less likely we are to destroy it.

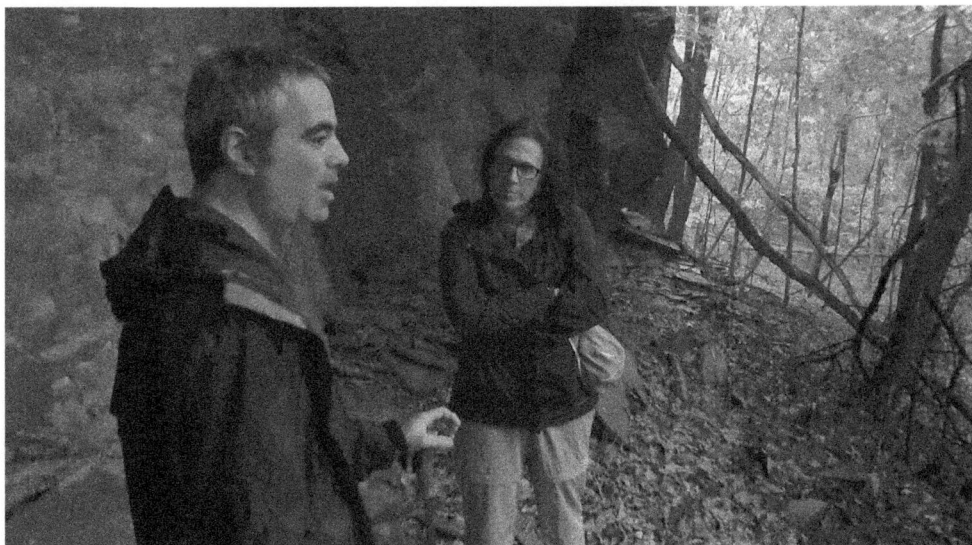

It was *pouring* rain during most of our hike, and Glenn and I take shelter for a few minutes under a rock overhang.
Mike stands by one of the large rock piles.

To learn more about this site and others in the region, read Glenn Kreisberg's upcoming book *Spirits in Stone*. To learn more about the Overlook Mountain Center's mission, educational programs and hiking tours, please visit www.overlookmountain.org.

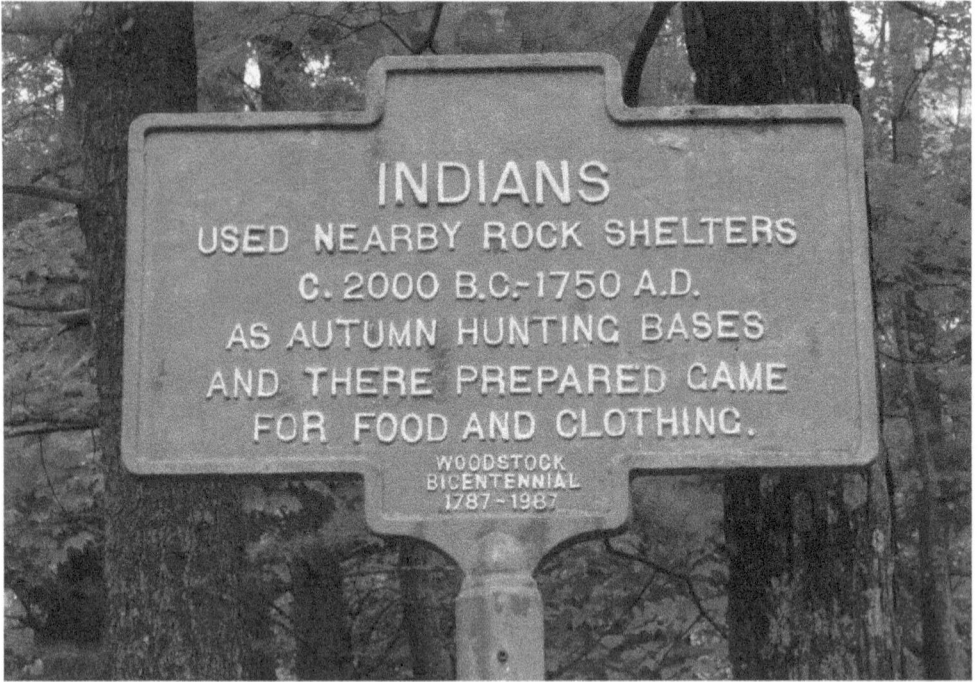

INDIANS
USED NEARBY ROCK SHELTERS
C. 2000 B.C.-1750 A.D.
AS AUTUMN HUNTING BASES
AND THERE PREPARED GAME
FOR FOOD AND CLOTHING.
WOODSTOCK
BICENTENNIAL
1787-1987

An historic marker nearby indicating thousands of years of Native American habitation in this area.
Standing on one of the huge rock piles.

John H. Bradner
1926-1998

John H. Bradner was a Warwick, New York resident who traveled the world, researching and photographing megalithic sites from Europe to Tasmania, but came to believe there were equally fascinating and historic sites literally in his own backyard.

I was able to study his research, thanks to the Bradner family, who donated his notebooks and photo albums to the Albert Wisner Public Library in Warwick. Reference librarian Sue Gardner made me aware of this collection, and I quickly arranged to view it.

As a child growing up in Warwick, Bradner used to play on a large, curious rock formation behind his house, known as Table Rock.

TABLE ROCK'S POSSIBLE ALTAR — A SEMI-CIRCULAR STONE TABLE PROTRUDING ABOUT 2' ABOVE PRESENT GROUND LEVEL. (NOTE WHITE STONE IN CENTER)

"I remembered when I started doing my research on megalithic structures in the 70s," Bradner said in an October 7, 1967 article in the *Times Herald Record* newspaper. "It occurred to me that maybe Table

133

Rock was a man-made formation, built by some Stone-Age culture. I did some work with another archaeologist. It took a long time to clean it all out and excavate it properly...I don't think it's a natural formation. It was definitely shaped by someone."

Table Rock is an 18-foot-high, 10-foot-square piece of limestone inside "a fortress-like configuration." Bradner found that by standing on some stone steps cut into the rock, winter solstice sunset could be seen through a crevice, lining up with a notch on the side of Table Rock.

Bradner extensively hiked through the Ramapos, Hudson Highlands, and Kittatinny Mountains and found many stone features he believed were man-made. He was greatly inspired by Barry Fell's book, *America, B.C.*, and definitely jumped on Fell's Celtic-Iberian bandwagon as to the origins of the builders of these sites. This obviously influenced Bradner's interpretations, such as in the case of the supposed "Druid Throne" he describes in the Warwick Valley. However, even if ancient European priests were not the builders, the stone sites remain important discoveries.

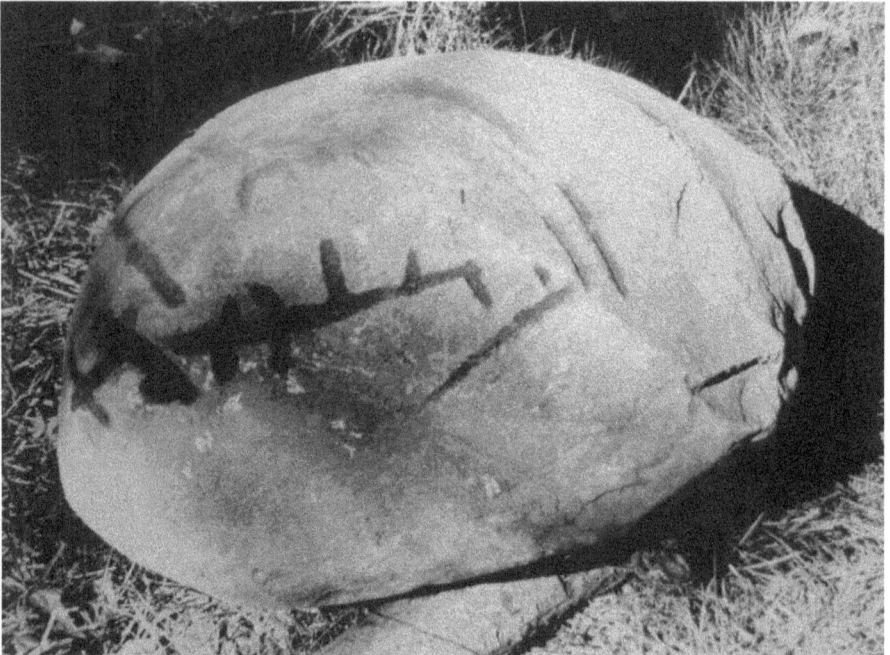

A rock Bradner found near the Doublekill creek near Warwick, NY which he
believed contained an ancient Ogam inscription.
He highlighted the lines with water.

One site that Bradner felt had particular significance was the former Luther Barrett Farm, which is now part of Wawayanda State Park in Passaic County, New Jersey. Bradner believed these 200 acres were "loaded with calendar sites," including a semi-circle of stones at the highest point, with inscribed compass points and a winter solstice sunset/summer solstice sunrise alignment. He admitted that this area was a "great mystery" with its many stone features and became "almost an obsession."

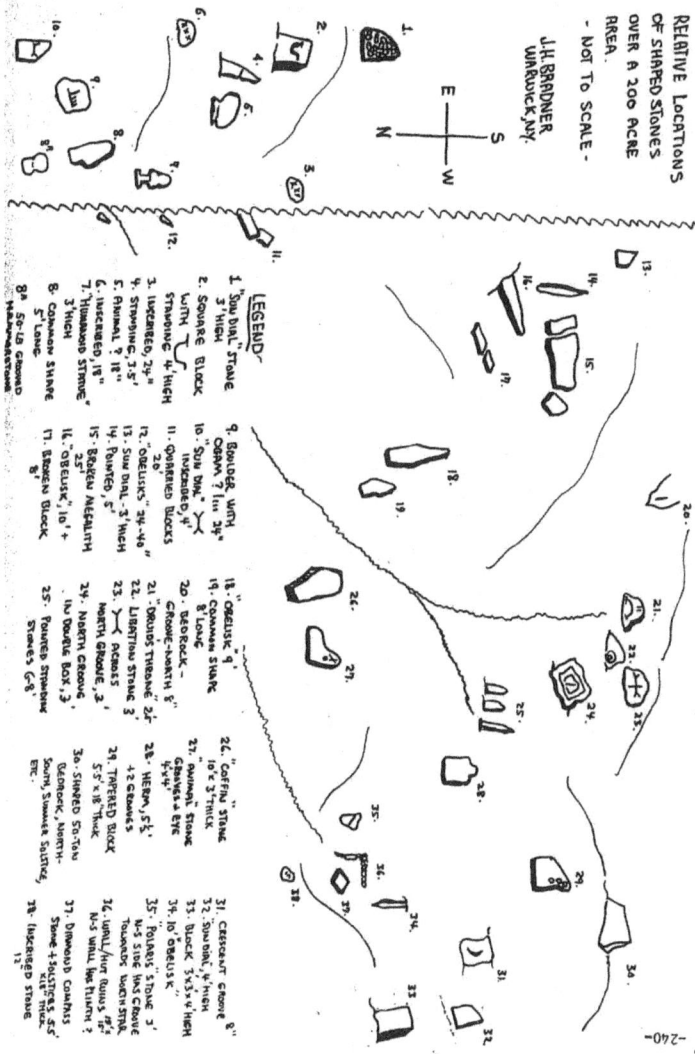

RELATIVE LOCATIONS OF SHAPED STONES OVER A 200 ACRE AREA.
- NOT TO SCALE -

J.H. BRADNER
WARWICK, N.Y.

LEGEND

1. "SUN DIAL" STONE 3' HIGH
2. SQUARE BLOCK WITH ⌣⌣ INSCRIBED
3. INSCRIBED, 2½'
4. STANDING 4' HIGH
5. ANIMAL ? 18"
6. POINTED, 5'
7. HUMPBACK STONE 3' THICK
8. COMMON SHAPE 5' LONG
8A. S? LG GROUND MANIPULATIONS

9. BOULDER WITH GROOVE ? 1" x 24"
10. "SUN DIAL" INSCRIBED, 4'
11. "QUARRIED BLOCKS" 2.6
12. "OBELISKS" 24'-40'
13. SUN DIAL - 3' HIGH
14. POINTED, 5'
15. BROKEN MEGALITH 25'
16. "OBELISK", 10'+
17. BROKEN BLOCK 8'

18. "OBELISK" 9'
19. COMMON SHAPE 8' LONG
20. BEDROCK -
21. "DRUIDS THRONE 2½' GROOVE-NORTH 8"
22. LIBATION STONE 2½'
23. ⌣ POINTS NORTH GROOVE,
24. NORTH GROOVE, 3'
25. POINTED STANDING STONES 6-8'

26. COFFIN STONE 10' x 3' THICK
27. ANIMAL STONE GROOVES + EYE 4'x4'
28. HERM, 5½' + 2 GRAVES
29. TAPERED BLOCK 5½' x 18" THICK
30. SHAPED SO-TOW BEDROCK, NORTH-SOUTH, SUMMER SOLSTICE, ETC.

31. CRESCENT GROOVE 8"
32. SUN DIAL, 4' HIGH
33. BLOCK 3'x3'x4' HIGH
34. 10' OBELISK
35. POLARIS STONE 3'
36. WALL/HUT RUINS N-S SIDE HAS GRAVE, TOWARDS NORTH STAR
37. DIAMOND COMPASS STONE + SOLSTICES 5½'x ? THICK
38. INSCRIBED STONE 12"

-240-

135

Another curious site studied by Bradner is Hickory Hill. Fortunately, much of this land is preserved in the Warwick County Park, although a good portion of it became a golf course. Bradner found several interesting stone features, including what he believed was a turtle effigy. Having been to the site, I do agree that it resembles a turtle, and the fact that is pointing due south, adds to the fact that it was something of significance.

Unfortunately, the book Bradner had been planning was never completed, but at least his notes and photographs remain. And many of the words of this world traveler and researcher remain, as well:

"The idea of man-made megaliths in North America is definitely a controversial subject. Most archaeologists don't acknowledge they exist. But I find it difficult to explain these formations any other way."

My photo of the turtle effigy at Hickory Hill.
Some of the stone artifacts Bradner found over the years.

Bradner also found these curious stones, one with "checkerboard" carvings.

Kingston Megaliths and Circles
Kingston, New York

In 2003, a proposed construction site in Kingston, New York was surveyed by the New York Old Growth Forest Association. Their job was to find "remnants of ancient forests"[1] in order to have those trees protected. Other than some old oaks, however, their survey didn't turn up anything of significance—unless you consider the massive standing stones.

Even the city of Kingston realized this was a man-made grouping of limestone megaliths. Their environmental impact study stated that this site was ancient, possibly Neolithic, and therefore, it should be preserved.

---

[1] *Kingston, New York Stonehenge?*, Crispin Kott, *Alternative Science and History News*, July14, 2008

These stones may be a calendar site, providing solstice sunrise alignments with the ridge to the east across the Hudson River. There may also have been other alignments with separate, smaller stones, but while the megaliths were preserved, the surrounding land was cleared for an industrial park. Any other possible features were obliterated—or were they?

Bob examines the megaliths.

Before visiting any site, I like to use Google Earth to get a bird's eye view of the area, and look for anything unusual. When looking over the land around Corporate Drive, where the megaliths are located, one feature popped into view in an open field on the northeast section of the parking area. It was a pair of concentric circles that stood out quite clearly. Could it be the remnants of an ancient stone or wood henge? Could it be the foundation of a colonial farmer's silo? Or, was it simply modern tire tracks from someone making "donuts" in the dirt? It was impossible to say from the photo, but it certainly made this site a lot more interesting.

As always, nothing beats having "boots on the ground," so to speak, so one day after doing a book signing at the Kingston Barnes and Noble, I went to Corporate Drive to find the megaliths. If you drive along the western side of the parking lot, you can't miss them, even with all the trees and undergrowth. These massive stones stick out like the proverbial sore thumb. It was difficult to get around them with all the tangled vines and bushes, but I was able to get some photos. More importantly, I was able to determine that a slot between two of the stones was basically aimed east-west, which could allow for the observation of equinox sunrise and sunset.

I next drove over to the field, but unfortunately, from the ground, I was unable to discern the concentric circles, which should have been quite large. This was either a transient feature, then, which washed or blew away, or it has since been covered in gravel. Or, it is one of those archaeological sites that can only be discerned with aerial photography?

Google Earth image of the mysterious concentric circles.

On a subsequent visit to the site a couple of years later, Bob noticed a massive rock standing on the edge of a ridge along Corporate Drive. While it does not appear to have been moved by the hand of man, it is positioned directly to the south of the mysterious circle, so if this was once a large calendar site, perhaps this rock played a role.

The list of curious sites in Kingston doesn't end here, however, as there is also a large stone circle—right next to the Hudson Valley Mall! I contacted the town historian for information about this circle, but unfortunately never received a response, so I have no official word as to what it is, or maybe more importantly, what it isn't.

Google Earth view of the circle, and my photo of it in the snow.

I visited the site on two separate occasions; once in deep snow, and another time when it was clear, and I took many photographs. Here's what I can say from my observations:

- The grooves and drill holes in the bedrock give indications that this was a quarry site for stone blocks, but the extreme weathering on the edges gives the appearance that it is a very old quarry. A geologist would be needed to determine the type of stone and its weathering patterns.

- Many of the stones in the circle have drill holes, but they don't appear to be clean, recent holes. It's not a perfect circle, either, and it is questionable as to why these stones would have been placed on top of the quarry grooves. Were the stones in a different arrangement or location, and moved by construction crews building the mall? Did someone with a bulldozer and a sense of humor think it would be fun to make a circle?

- The large standing stone also shows multiple drill marks, and is also highly weathered. Is this an ancient alignment stone, or just another big rock moved by construction crews?

Without additional information, I can only say that this is a curious feature where some stone working has been done in the past. How far in the past, of course, is the question.

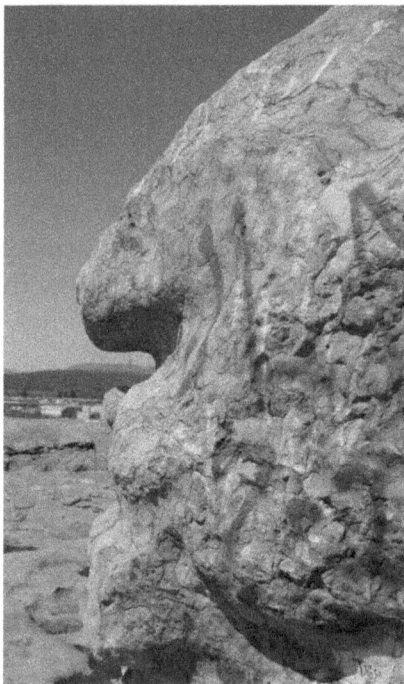

Bob next to the large standing stone, and a close up of a groove on the side.

These sites in Kingston are three more locations to be added to the list for future study, and I hope local historians and scientists will look into them. As calendar sites or ceremonial places often involve great sections of landscape, it is impossible to see the entire puzzle with only a handful of pieces, but that doesn't mean we shouldn't try.

Note: As of summer 2017, this site was slated for development with a bar/restaurant. The developer claims he will preserve the stone features.

Indian Dam
Plattekill, New York

According to one of the first settlers in Plattekill, NY in the early 1700s, he came upon a huge stone wall that appeared to be ancient. As the wall was in the midst of a swampy area, the settlers called it the Indian Dam, as they assumed the local Native American population had labored to construct it many years earlier. They may be correct about the builders, but its purpose doesn't seem to be that of a dam—or anything else that historians can imagine.

One of the best descriptions of the Indian Dam is from *Legends of the Shawangunks*, written by Philip Smith in 1887:

One of the greatest curiosities, in point of the mysteriousness of its origin in the county of Ulster, is that bit of ancient masonry in the town of Plattekill known as the "Indian Dam." It is located on what is known as the Levi Bodine farm, now occupied by J.S. Terwiliger, Jr. The dam in question consists of two stone walls joined at an obtuse angle, and it is about one hundred and fifty yards in length, eight or ten feet in height at the highest part, and four feet in width at the top. It is built across a stream at the outlet of a heavily timbered swamp, and would submerge about one hundred acres. As there is scarcely any perceptible fall, the dam could hardly have been built to furnish water power, hence the question as to the purpose of its construction has never been satisfactorily answered. What is stranger still, when the first settlers came into the vicinity, more than a century ago, the dam was there in the same condition in which it is now found; nor could they ascertain when, by whom, or for what purpose it was built. Though called the Indian Dam, it is not probable the Indians had anything to do with its construction, as they were not given to wall-building. Its origins may have been coeval with that of the ancient roads in the vicinity of the Shawangunk mountain, called the "Mine Roads," indications of which may yet be seen at various points at the foot of the declivities on either side, of which neither history nor tradition can give a satisfactory answer.

Despite Smith's belief that Indians could not possibly have been the builders, he does make it clear that these walls were here long before the settlers arrived. Who, then, were these mystery builders? He doesn't know, but he suggests that they may have been the same group of people who also built the old roads.

Shifting the origin of the walls back into the Native American's court was Sal Trento and his MARC[2] team. During their study of the site, they took aerial photographs, which they claimed showed a faint trail leading directly from the Indian Dam eastward—right to the Danskammer on the Hudson River. The Danskammer was the spot in 1609 where Henry Hudson and the Dutch sailors witnessed the Wappinger Indians conducting ceremonies in which they danced and chanted to their god, Bachtamo. To the Dutch, these were savage rituals to the devil, hence the name *De Duyfel's Dans Kammer*, or the Devil's Dance Chamber. (This site now contains a massive power generating plant.)

Of course there are, shall we say, unconventional explanations for the Indian Dam, as well. In 1979, a dowser, Don Wood, claimed that by using his dowsing rods he was able to determine that 2,650 years ago, white men came from Wales and built the walls. They lived there for 67 years, and used the walls for astrology.

Other theories have also been put forth, and there has been some suggestion that this site might be somehow connected to the Poughkeepsie Standing Stone and a site in Ellenville. The bottom line, however, is that there is no definitive proof as to who built the walls, why they were built, or when they were built. As Philip Smith so aptly phrased it, there is a great "mysteriousness" about the Indian Dam.

I was most anxious to visit this site myself, and the Plattekill Town Historian, Elizabeth Werlau, and Shirley Anson of the Plattekill Historical Society were both very helpful in supplying me with articles, along with the contact information of the current owner of the property. I wrote to the owner requesting permission to view the Indian Dam, but did not receive a response. Obviously, if this is private property, I will not trespass on it. But it is a great shame that such an important site is closed to research.

---

[2] The Middletown Archaeological Research Center, or MARC, was a private organization formed to study sites in the Northeast during the 1970s. I contacted Salvatore Trento a few years ago in hopes that he still had the valuable MARC files on all of these sites. At the time, he was on an underwater archaeological expedition off the Yucatan Peninsula, and had no idea what happened to the files. If anyone knows of their whereabouts, please contact me.

For now, the mystery of the Indian Dam will have to remain unsolved. However, I think it is safe to say that such a major undertaking of labor means that this was a very special place to whatever group of people constructed it.

Poughkeepsie Standing Stone
Delavergne Avenue, Wappingers Falls, NY

I love Google Maps. With the power of online reconnaissance, you can be an armchair history detective and cover more ground in a few minutes than you could in a few days. I often use Google Maps to get an idea of the surrounding area of a site I want to visit, but it's even more helpful when I can use it to actually *find* a site.

Such was the case with the so-called "Poughkeepsie Standing Stone." For many years I had seen the occasional photo or sketch, and had inquired with local history resources, but no one could tell me *where* it was. Sal Trento's book, *The Search for Lost America*, had a description and sketch of the stone, and a simple map showing its relative position to the northeast of a hill somewhere between the NY Central Railroad tracks and the Wappinger Creek, which left a lot of ground to search.

I decided to use Google Maps to see if I could find any of the features, and quickly determined the general area, which happened to actually be in Wappingers Falls, not Poughkeepsie. There was indeed a hill—a hill that has the sprawling 204-acre Mt. Alvernia Retreat Center. To make matters worse, from an archaeological perspective, there were housing developments stretching along the entire length of the other side of the road, where the map indicated the standing stone should be. My heart sank—what developer would leave a huge standing stone in the middle of his development? Maybe this was why no one could tell me where it was, because it had been yanked out of the ground and dumped somewhere.

Still, it was worth hopping into my virtual car and driving down Delavergne Avenue on Google Maps past Mt. Alvernia. I hadn't "driven" more than two mouse clicks when I saw something odd sticking up out of the ground at the corner of Oakwood Drive. Could it really be that easy?

Another two clicks and there was the distinctive stone on someone's green lawn, still intact! I was delighted that it was still in one piece, in its original location. And don't let just this few feet of stone sticking out fool you—tests have shown that it is actually a whopping 18 feet long! More of the standing stone used to be visible, but several feet of dirt were added by a previous land owner to level the property. And who knows how much of it has been covered over the centuries?

Google Maps image of standing stone on right.

Here are some of the facts about this standing stone: It was already there when the earliest Dutch settlers arrived, so it was not placed there by colonial hands. This area was a very important governing and religious center to the Wappinger Indians. The stone itself shows signs of having been worked, so it is not a creation of nature.

While the Wappinger Indians or other Native Americans would have

been more than capable of placing this stone, it should be pointed out that it is also reminiscent of the *menhirs* of Europe and Asia, particularly those in Ireland, Great Britain, and France. Of course in those countries, menhirs are respected as ancient monuments, while here they are ignored and overlooked.

© Photo of menhir in Devon, Great Britain, copyright Rowena Ford and licensed for reuse under the Creative Commons License.

The Mine Hole
Piermont, NY

Abandoned mine shafts generally don't arouse much interest—unless there are absolutely no clues as to when and why one was excavated, and who did all the digging. Such is the case with the Mine Hole in Piermont by the Sparkill Creek. The shaft extends back into the mountain for a distance of about 100 feet, with an average width of five feet and a height of about six feet. The tunnel begins by heading north, turns ninety degrees to the west and eventually leads to a dead end. However, just past the turn there is a small hole leading to a ten-foot square room. Speculations about the origins of the Mine Hole have ranged from a simple attempt by colonists to find useful or valuable minerals, to a Viking storehouse.

What is known for certain is that by the time of the Revolutionary War, the Mine Hole already existed, as soldiers in the area had written about it. However, whether the tunnel had been dug ten years earlier, a hundred years earlier, or even longer is anybody's guess.

By the early 1900s, the Mine Hole had become a tourist destination. This, in part, was because of the natural spring that flowed from it. An inscription beckoned the thirsty:

O Traveler
Stay thy Weary feet
Drink of this fountain cool and sweet, it
Flows for man and beast the same
Then on thy way remembering
Still, the well beneath the hill

Not surprisingly, the original plaque was stolen, but was finally replaced in 1976. Unfortunately by that point, the pure mountain spring water had long since been contaminated, and the entrance had been sealed in 1943, due to a cave-in that occurred as sewer lines were being constructed on the mountain above the old mine shaft.

Even though you can no longer venture into the dark recesses of the Mine Hole, it's worth stopping to take and look and let your imagination go to work. Did some early Dutch or English settler use gunpowder to blast through the solid rock, in search of iron, silver, or gold? Had it been raw muscle power—Viking muscle power—that slowly chipped a tunnel to nowhere? Or was it some sort of Native American ceremonial site? Without further investigation, it is all pure speculation. Until then, it is unlikely that the Mine Hole will ever reveal its secrets.

The Mine Hole as it looks today, across from 175 Piermont Avenue.

150

Stone Pillar
Washington Road, Carmel NY

While going through the Delong-Cooke Stone Structure Map, I came upon the following entry for a site on Washington Road in Carmel, New York, on the west side of the West Branch Reservoir:

Stone Pillar on Reservoir side with two holes 72" apart. It has perfect N-S, E-W alignment even allowing for declination from magnetic north.

I was intrigued by a pillar tall enough to have holes six feet apart, and thought that this must be a large, impressive pillar—and one that was even aligned to the cardinal points! In September of 2015, Mike and I were in the Carmel area looking at some stone chambers, and decided to try to find this pillar. Coordinates had been supplied in the Delong-Cooke listing, so I put them in my GPS unit and we headed down Washington Avenue.

The woods here are thick, and the undergrowth was even thicker, but we pushed our way through to the location indicated by the coordinates. At any moment, I fully expected to turn and find a massive column of stone, but we found nothing. Giving some slack to the coordinates, we went in opposite directions and zig-zagged back and forth to cover as much ground as possible. An occasional tree stump in the distance fooled me for a second, but no tall pillars of stone were to be found.

We were determined however, and kept going a little further down the road to continue our search pattern. Still nothing. I admit I was ready to give up, but Mike wanted to try one more spot, just north of a little creek, which wasn't even close to the coordinates, but it was worth a try if we could find this towering pillar.

"There it is!" Mike exclaimed, about ten seconds after getting out of the car.

Excited, I turned to look where he was pointing, but all I saw were trees.

"Where?" I asked, incredulous that I couldn't see a column of stone large enough to have holes six feet apart.

Mike pointed again, and I realized he wasn't pointing up high. Dropping my eyes downward, I finally saw the stone pillar, standing only a little more than three feet high! I began to wonder if any of the information about this pillar was correct.

The first thing I noticed was that it did have two sets of holes, but obviously not six feet apart, more like two feet. Holding my GPS unit by the top set of holes, which went clear through the pillar, it was a perfect east-west sightline, and the other axis of the stone pointed north-south. This alignment added weight to the idea that it was an old, possibly ancient, trail marker, but something about the holes bothered me.

When I got home and examined the photos, I saw that the camera flash had revealed a circular, reddish, discoloration around the top holes, as if there had been iron fittings rusting in them, like those used for hitching posts. But why would a simple hitching post be oriented so precisely? Had this been an ancient trail marker, and a more recent farmer decided to drill a hole in it to make a hitching post?

This site becomes even more interesting when you consider the fact that there is a stone chamber close-by, just across the road. Unfortunately, due to the dense vegetation and not wanting to trespass on private property, we were unable to see this chamber from the street, so we couldn't tell if it was modern or old.

There is also a long stone wall that runs behind a cemetery a short distance to the south, which may have been from a farm, but there's another curious row of large stones that runs perpendicular to it. Heading from west to east, this row of stones look as though they were interrupted by the road, and may have stretched farther east. With the creation of the reservoir, some features may now be underwater.

It would, of course, be helpful to be able to examine the stone chamber near the pillar, and determine if it, too, has any special alignment. It would also be interesting to try to find out just how long the stone pillar actually is—could we only be seeing its tip?

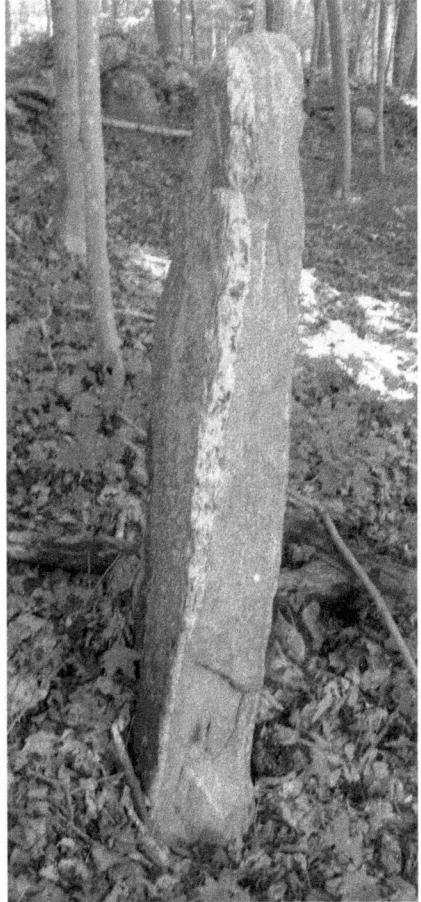

The southwest edge of the pillar has a vein of white quartz.

Once again, we have yet another site with more questions than answers…

<u>Stone Pillar Coordinates</u>: N 41.41292, W 073.70987

Please note: Like the Whangtown Road chambers site, you need a NYC Watershed Permit to access this site. While the pillar can be seen from the road, if you want to explore it up close and the surrounding woods you must have a permit. When Mike and I were there, a police car did come by, so it's not worth the risk, especially since the permits are free. Please go to their website for more information and to obtain a permit.

http://www.nyc.gov/html/dep/html/watershed_protection/recreation.shtml

The row of large stones running east-west.

Spook Rock and Indian Rock
Airmont and Montebello, NY

Spook Rock in Airmont, New York, is one of many large stones and glacial erratics that have acquired fanciful legends and ghost stories. Over the generations, stories about Spook Rock have undergone so many variations that only three elements remain consistent—Native Americans, a rock, and a ghost.

Spook is an old Dutch term meaning spirit, and the primary tale also involves some of the earliest Dutch settlers in the county. As the story goes, one of the settlers committed some kind of crime against the local Indian population—something even worse than the usual ill treatment native peoples often received. Whatever the deed, the result was that the long-suffering Indians decided to seek revenge. They kidnapped the young daughter of the offending settler and brought her to the rocky site they used for ceremonies. At the time, there was supposedly a cave beneath the rock, and the rock itself had a large indentation that would have been ideal for a bonfire.

After conducting the appropriate revenge ceremony, the innocent girl was sacrificed on the rock. Almost immediately after the terrible deed was done, members of the tribe learned that the settler was not guilty of the crime for which he had been accused. This left the chief with unbearable feelings of guilt and remorse, and some versions of the story say that the ghost of the murdered girl, visible only to the chief, haunted him every night for the rest of his life. There is also a version that claims that the girl's spirit was seen by all of the members of the tribe, hovering over the rock where her unjust death occurred.

There are countless other versions, but spooky legends aside, the important thing here is that this is a large rock considered to be an Indian ceremonial site even in the time of the early Dutch colonists. At the very least, local historians think that Spook Rock was a marker along the trail which various tribes took to gather in Mahwah, New Jersey. The word "Mahwah" is believed to mean "meeting place."

Unfortunately, Spook Rock has been altered over the years, and with the intrusion of Spook Rock Road, a masonry wall had to be constructed to keep it from rolling into the street. It's impossible to know what it looked like before the colonists arrived, and whether or not there were any other stone features in the surrounding landscape, but at least we know there was one rock used as a sign post, and perhaps much more.

Along that same trail to Mahwah is the more massive and impressive Indian Rock. In the 1990s, the land upon which this rock had sat for many thousands of years was sold to a developer—with the agreement that the rock remain intact. However, once the developer began clearing the site, he decided the rock was just too much in the way and planned to renege on his agreement and break it to pieces. Fortunately, thanks to a groundswell of local support, Indian Rock was saved. The shopping center eventually went up around the rock, which is now enclosed in a fence to prevent people from climbing on top, or from crawling into the opening inside of the rock, which may have once acted as a shelter.

(An interesting note: despite wanting to pulverize the rock, the new development decided to take the name Indian Rock Shopping Center! If you can't beat them, join them, I guess.)

In any event, both rocks have been preserved and stand as evidence that Native Americans most likely used them for navigation, for meeting places, for shelter, and perhaps many other things. Someday, Spook Rock and Indian Rock might also be recognized in a much wider landscape of trails and ceremonial sites.

Spook Rock is by the corner of Spook Rock Road in Airmont, NY, by the intersection with North Airmont Road. Indian Rock Shopping Center is on Route 59 in Montebello, near the intersection of Hemion Road.

M.I.A.
(Missing In Archaeology)

The following are sites whose whereabouts are currently unknown, and may have been destroyed. Any further information on these sites would be appreciated.

The Missing Stonehenge?
Hudson, New York

In *The American Journal of Science and Arts*, Volume 7, published in 1824, John Finch wrote in his article, *On the Celtic Antiquities of America*:

> *3. Circles of Memorial* were the next monuments erected by the ancient Celtæ ; they consist of nine, twelve, or more rude stones, placed so as to form a circle, and were generally placed upon an eminence.
>
> They answered several purposes; they were dedicated to religious services, and sacrifices were made either within the sacred circle, or in its vicinity ; at the election of chiefs and leaders, the nations assembled here, and public business was supposed to be sanctioned by the gods, if transacted within the boundary of their temples. They were also used by the priests for astronomical purposes.
>
> There appear to be at least three of these sacred circles in America. I have been informed of one by Dr F. James, the scientific tourist to the Rocky Mountains. It is situated upon a high hill. one mile from the town of Hudson, in the State of New-York, and attracted his notice many years ago, on account of the remarkable size of the stones, and their position.

Finch was a British geologist who had no doubt that the stone sites he was seeing in America were constructed by the same people who built similar ancient structures in his homeland. (See Dolmens and Perched Boulders chapter.) His source for the account of this amazing circle of massive stones in Hudson, NY, was an American scientist of great distinction—Dr. Edwin James: botanist, geologist, and the first man to climb Pike's Peak in Colorado. (General Zebulon Pike, for whom the mountain is named, actually failed in his attempt to climb the peak.)

Dr. James was a keen observer, so if he saw a circle of stones of "remarkable size," it should be considered a credible report. But where is this circle today? I contacted the Columbia County Historical Society with this information, which apparently created quite a stir amongst the local historians. Unfortunately, however, despite their interest, they had never heard of this circle of stones.

On the one hand, I was confident in the source of the information, yet equally confident that if it still existed, the Historical Society would know about it. I had to come to the sad conclusion that this archaeological treasure has been destroyed.

There had been some speculation that the massive circle of stones was on Mt. Merino, and when the power lines cut a swath over the mountains the site was bulldozed. It is a sickening thought, but unfortunately, such acts of destruction have been commonplace across the American landscape for centuries. We can only hope that any further loss of such sites can be avoided.

Google Maps image of the power lines and towers on Mt. Merino.

Stone Circle
Rea Court, Monroe, NY

At the end of Rea Court in Monroe, NY, there is—or was—a 20-foot diameter stone circle. The stones are—or were—each about one or two feet in diameter.

As this location is not far from where I live, as soon as I read about it in Salvatore Trento's book, *Field Guide to Mysterious Places in Eastern North America*, I took a drive to Rea Court and slowly went back and forth, trying not to look as though I was up to some sort of criminal activity. I was unable to see any stone circles, or anything at all unusual. Google Maps also failed to reveal any circles in the heavily-wooded residential area.

In a final attempt, I wrote a letter describing my project and included the reference to Trento's book. I went back to Rea Court and placed a copy of this letter in every mailbox, hoping someone could shed some light on the stone circle. No one responded.

Does the 20-foot circle still exist in someone's backyard, or was it destroyed for a house or pool, or just because it was in the way?

Peekskill Rocking Stone
Oscawanna Lake Road, Putnam Valley, NY?

In 1824, John Finch wrote about another stone curiosity in the Hudson Valley—a massive, moveable, 30-foot-diameter, half-round piece of granite resting in a sort of stone cradle, "situated near the top of a high hill near the village of Peekskill." It was Finch's opinion that the rocking stone was not natural, that it had been placed there. He reported that one man had the ability to make the huge stone move, yet six men with crowbars were unable to dislodge it—although why they even tried to destroy such an amazing site is beyond me!

I contacted the Field Library in Peekskill to see if I could locate the Rocking Stone, and Robert Boyle and Kim Stucko were very helpful providing whatever information they had, but we couldn't pin down the exact spot. I also posted the image of the stone on my Mysterious Hudson Valley Stone Sites Facebook page, and Martin Brech was kind enough to share a c. 1940 map by historian Allison Albee which shows the location of the Rocking Stone somewhere to the east of the north end of Lake Oscawanna, but with the old roads it was confusing.

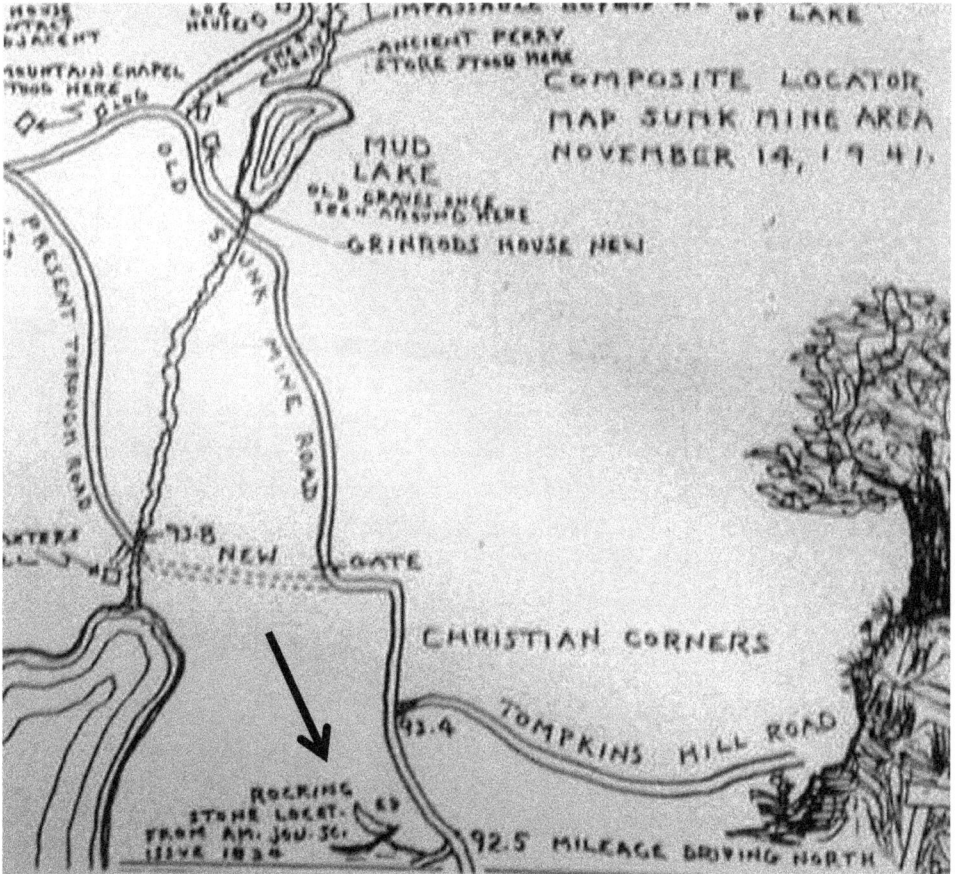

Brech informed me that "Tompkins Hill Road is now called Oscawanna Heights Road", and "the road running south from Christian Corners is Oscawanna Lake Road." If so, this would place the Rocking Stone on someone's private property. I hope the owner of that property will allow researchers to examine this stone so that they can determine whether it is a curious freak of nature, or an incredible feat of ancient engineering.

Balance Rock
South Nyack, NY

BALANCE ROCK, SOUTH MOUNTAIN, SO. NYACK, N. Y.

I don't know why it is that people feel compelled to destroy things, but such was the case with Balance Rock in South Nyack, NY. The 22-foot boulder was a local attraction which gained more widespread interest when it was featured in several post cards in the early 1900s.

In the 1950s, some seniors at the local high school decided that for their class prank they would push the boulder over the edge of the mountain. About 15 students showed up and failed miserably. It was later determined that given the weight of the enormous boulder and the way it was positioned in a crevice, it would have taken about 2,000 students to dislodge it and roll it over the edge.

Of course, where one group of stupid students failed, other groups thought they would succeed. Each successive graduating class tried to push Balance Rock off its perch, where it had sat since the last glacier receded. Finally, word spread one year that students from all over the area were going to get dozens, perhaps hundreds, of people to try to push the stone. Fearing that the dislodged boulder would come barreling down South Mountain and destroy the entire village below, local cops were dispatched to thwart the attempt.

Apparently, however, ongoing fears of a rolling rock Armageddon led to Balance Rock's ultimate demise in December of 1965. Without the public's knowledge, the rock was dynamited into little pieces.

If Balance Rock was part of any celestial alignments, the chance to study it was lost when the rock was blown apart.

Greenwood Balanced Rock
Greenwood Lake, NJ?

GREENWOOD BALANCED ROCK [CUT-A-WAY]
POINTED DUE NORTH WITH COUNTER-BALANCE SLAB

This photograph was in one of John Bradner's notebooks, but unfortunately he didn't give its location. If this precariously perched boulder still exists, it may be somewhere in the woods near Greenwood Lake in New Jersey. Have you seen it, or do you know where it is?

Winter Solstice Stones
Ladentown, NY?

In Trento's book, *Search for Lost America*, he describes a site supposedly on a ledge on Circle Mountain in Ladentown, NY. Three perched stones, one of which had fallen, would have formed an equilateral triangle, with a winter solstice sunset alignment occurring over the tall, center stone.

I was unable to find the location, so I consulted with Rockland County Historian Craig Long. He had not heard of this site either. In fact, we couldn't even find this alleged Circle Mountain. Obviously, Trento and the MARC team studied this site and produced a sketch of it, but must have been mistaken about the name of the mountain, and perhaps even the town.

The following is my crude sketch based on the information in the book. I would appreciate any information as to this site's whereabouts.

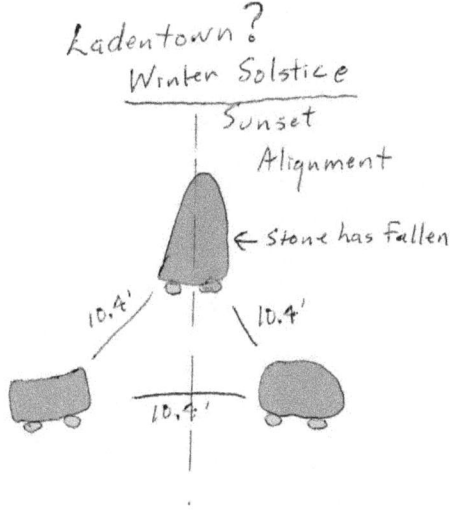

Winter Solstice Site
Greenwood Lake, NY or NJ?

This is another site mentioned in *Search for Lost America*. It contains a perched boulder and a semi-circle of stones, one of which has an inscription. There is both a winter solstice sunrise and sunset alignment. It is located somewhere near Greenwood Lake, but an exact location was not given.

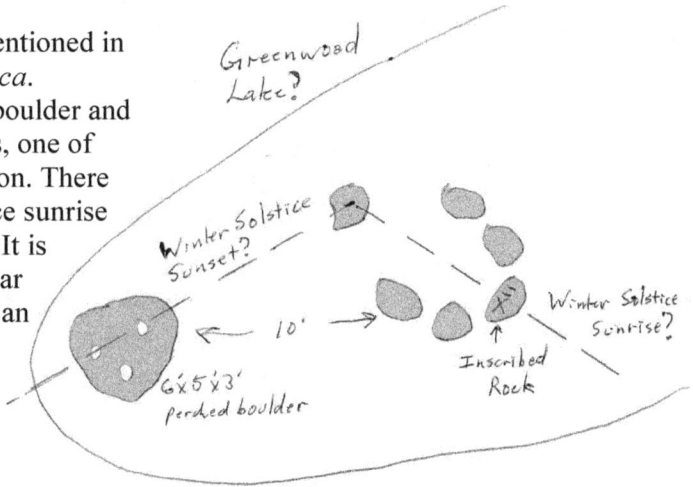

Circles of Stone
Palisades Interstate Park, NY or NJ?

This photo was in John Bradner's notebook. It has the labels "Winter Solstice Stone" and "Stone Circles Palisades I.P." No other information was provided.

Stone Cairns
Ellenville and Cornwall, NY

I have seen numerous references, photos, and illustrations of multiple stone cairns located in the towns of Ellenville and Cornwall, but no one has given exact locations. The Ellenville cairns are located somewhere off Route 209, and may have been destroyed by a housing development. The Cornwall cairns have been described as being on a hillside by a lake, near U.S. Military Academy property.

Do any of these cairns still exist?

Treasure Rock
Letterrock Mountain, Harriman State Park, NY

There are many legends of a treasure in silver involving Letterrock Mountain, and an arrowhead-shaped rock with inscriptions that pointed to the cave where it was hidden. This has led to a lot of treasure hunters over the years, but none more determined than the group of men in 1934 who used dynamite to blast away at the mountain looking for the silver bars and coins. Needless to say, they were arrested.

Letterrock was also said to contain a more ancient inscription, perhaps a Native American petroglyph of the rising sun. Were there other signs that this was a ceremonial area?

Bob and I hiked Letterrock Mountain several times and scoured the area for any signs of inscriptions, but found none. What we did find on the top of the mountain were these crescent-shaped marks in the bedrock. Though often mistaken for man-made carvings, they are, in fact, glacial "chatter marks"—a series of gouges left by rocks being dragged at the base of the glacier.

I also came across this interesting turtle-shaped, perched rock. In northeastern Native American creation myths, the world came into being on the back of a turtle, so it was an important symbol to them. I thought this was an even finer example than the turtle effigy at Hickory Hill in Warwick, NY. Note the rounded "head" peeking out on the left.

Do Native American petroglyphs or stone treasure maps still exist on Letterrock Mountain, or were they blown up in 1934? Regardless, this is yet one more area that needs to be studied for ceremonial or astronomical features.

New Discoveries at the Ramapo Walls

Several months after the first edition of this book was published in May of 2016, I was studying the site map to gather additional information. Until you have walked the length and breadth of the Ramapo Walls, you can't appreciate the scale of the entire site.

To quantify some of the distances, I measured the length from the fireplace to the highest mound on the map, and then used the scale of one inch equaling 290 feet to determine that it was about 471 feet. That didn't have any particular significance to me, but I jotted it down and went on to the next measurement. (Note: As I was using a copy of the map and not the original, I was working on the premise that it had been reproduced to scale. From the measurements I have personally taken at the site, these numbers are reasonably accurate.)

Placing the ruler between the fireplace and the 24-foot-diameter Pleiades mound, I performed the calculations and again came up with a distance of 471 feet.

I think I froze like a statue for a few moments. Had I mixed up my numbers and reentered the first set of figures? Rechecking, twice, I found there had been no mistake—*the distance between the fireplace and the highest mound was the same as the distance between the fireplace and the Pleiades mound*. Was this just an amazing coincidence, or was something else going on here—something that would prove once and for all that this was a highly sophisticated and planned site?

My heart beat a little faster as I measured and calculated the distance from the fireplace to the 30-foot-diameter Pleiades mound—471 feet. The distance from the fireplace to the southernmost 40-foot-diameter mound was also 471 feet. Measuring mound to mound, I found distances of 471 feet not in just one or two cases, but four.

Spreading out across the site, I found example after example of the same 471-foot unit of measurement repeated over and over between mounds, boulders, and bends and features in the walls. By the time I was done, I had discovered an astounding 37 examples of 471-foot lengths used in construction and placement! *Clearly, some standard unit of measure was used to plan out the entire site, and not one single feature was random—this was a mathematical masterpiece.*

169

My head was reeling as I contemplated the implications, and I actually laughed out loud at the previous theories that this site was the act of a farmer randomly tossing stones to clear his field. But I didn't stop there, as I reasoned that if a standard unit of measurement had been employed, 471 feet is a rather lengthy unit. What would I find if I looked for fractions of that unit?

Dividing 471 in half, I looked for any features that were about 235 feet apart. Once again, I found that four of the Pleiades mounds had been placed 235 feet apart. Searching the remainder of the site, I found a total of 20 of the same distances between mounds, boulders, and wall features.

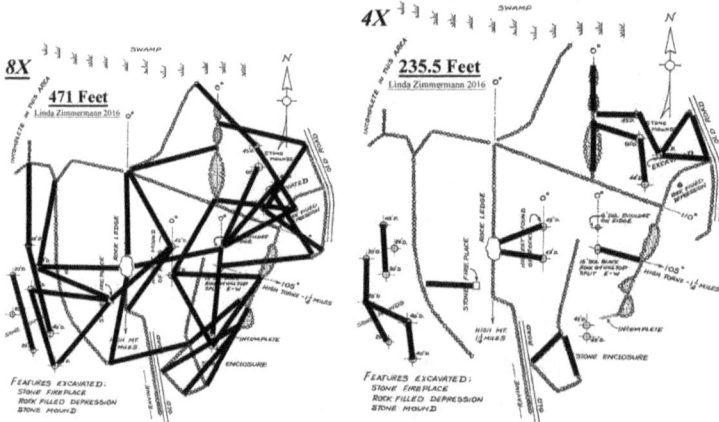

Next came half of 235, or about 117 feet. (Obviously, using a relatively small 8.5" by 11" map with a regular ruler, I was unable to exactly measure 117 feet, but it was easy to just keep dividing my measuring unit in half. Also, there was the question of where to begin and end a measurement, for example, at the center or edge of the mound or boulder?) This time there were 5 distances of 117 feet between the Pleiades mounds, with a total of 22 throughout the site.

The 117-foot measurement may also be the unit upon which the entire system was based, as the rock ledge near the center of the site is 117 feet long. As this is the one natural feature on the site—the one feature that was not manmade or positioned—it seems likely that the builders chose this as their "standard," rather than it being a complete coincidence that it falls into the master plan with such accuracy.

The smallest distance I was able to determine, given the map and ruler I was using, was half of 117, or about 59 feet. There were 9 features utilizing this shortest of the common units of measurements.

Going the opposite direction, I next looked for twice the distance of 471 feet, or 942 feet. Immediately, I saw that the longest single section of wall was indeed 942 feet! However, this time there were an impressive 27 total examples of this long unit of measurement stretching out across the entire site. How were the builders able to so accurately measure such distances over such uneven terrain, and often without a direct line of sight from point to point?

Towards the end of this initial phase of measurements and discovery, I came to realize that there was a key to this site, much like the information contained in the legends on a map. Just as those little boxes on a modern map provide the scales, orientations, etc. to unlock useful data, so, too, does the Ramapo Walls site have a key or legend—the three unique, pointed ellipses—a shape called a lens in geometry.

For starters, these lenses are oriented exactly north-south, so once you have found these features you know the orientation of the crucial cardinal points. In addition, the length and width of the lenses utilizes the standard units of measure. The lengths of the two smaller lenses are each 117 feet; half the size of the larger one, which is 235 feet. The widths of the two smaller lenses is about 59 feet, the smallest of the units of measure.

Therefore, once you for familiarize yourself with the lens key, you will know the units of measure upon which the entire site was planned out and constructed, as well as where to find the cardinal points. Was this the first feature constructed to give the builders a constant frame of reference, or was it a later addition for visitors to use to help navigate the site?

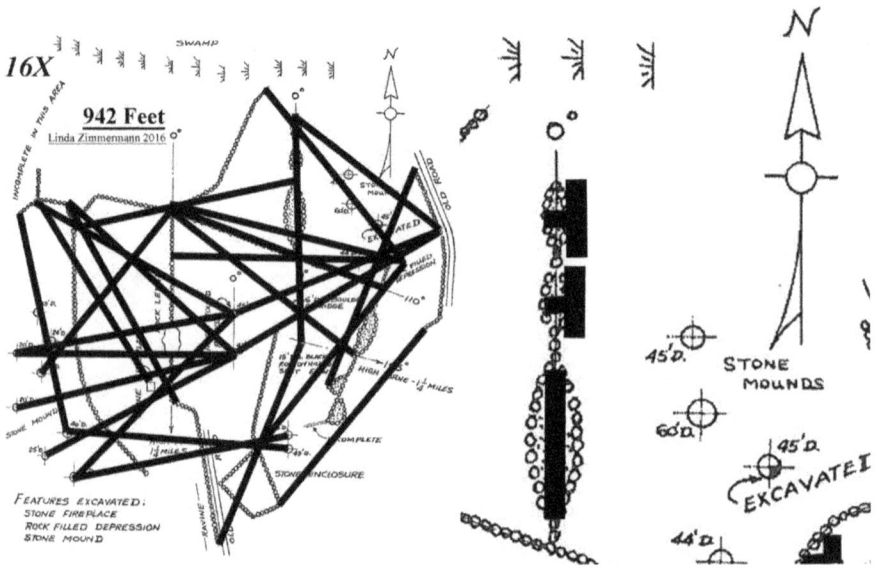

Over the following months, I delved deeper into the distances and relationships between the features. Knowing that triangles and unique ratios are also part of the geometry of ceremonial or sacred sites around the world, I found 3 equilateral triangles and 7 isosceles triangles between mound and wall features.

Possibly even more remarkable, is that the ratio of the distance between the fireplace, three of the Pleiades mounds, and the curved stone wall between them, may yield about 0.62—the Golden Ratio. This ratio is also found in the center of the site three times, with the highest stone mound, its partner due south, and the two prominent boulders.

Finally, the distance from the eastern to western limits of the site is the same as the northern to southern extent, at 2,030 feet, with the center of the "X" these lines form falling next to the highest mound on the site. (While this doesn't fit into the standard units of measure, it is unlikely to be a coincidence that these distances match.)

Based upon this overwhelming wealth of astronomical and mathematical data, it is my opinion that the Ramapo Walls are *the most important historical site* in Rockland County, the Hudson Valley, possibly New York State, and even much of New England. I call upon—in fact, I challenge--historians, archaeologists, astronomers, surveyors, and

172

mathematicians to leave behind their outdated, preconceived notions of stone sites in the Northeast and look at the preponderance of evidence here.

I can't say what groups of people calculated and constructed the alignments, distances, and positions of all the stone features, but I believe they were most likely Native Americans, possibly beginning construction around 1000 AD, based upon the alignment of the setting of the Pleiades over the stone mounds. Such a feat of planning and construction certainly wouldn't have been beyond the Mississippians or the Hopewell, so such sites are not without precedents in North America.

Regardless of the "who and when," we have the facts of the "what and where"—a 200-acre site of precisely measured, aligned, and positioned stone walls, mounds, and boulders. Isn't that enough to spark anyone's curiosity?

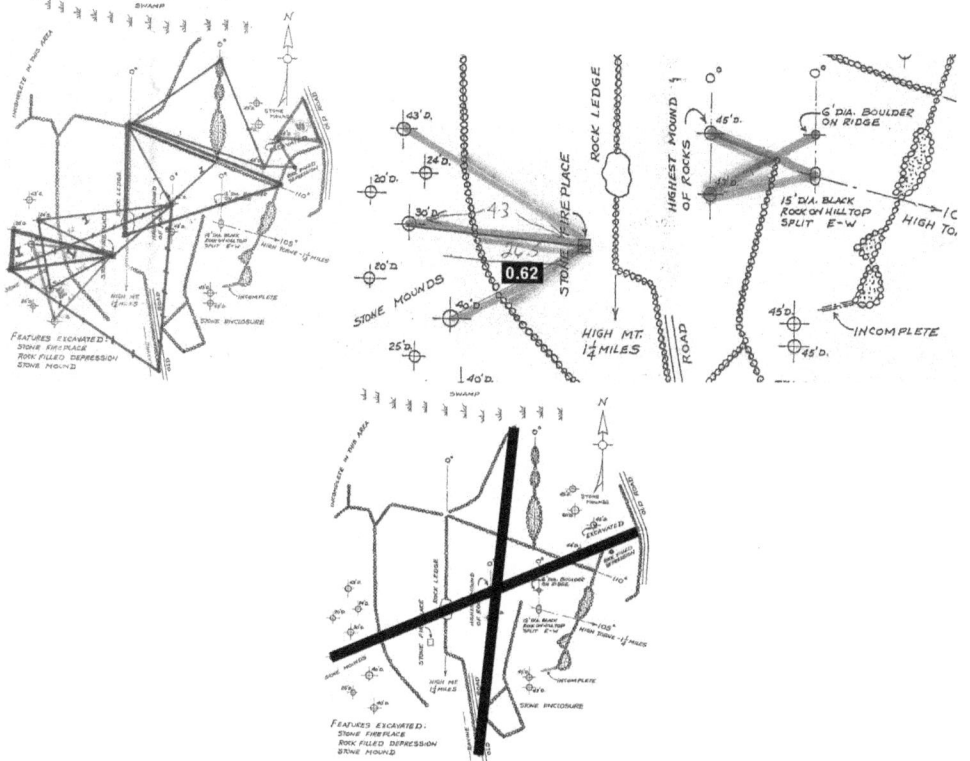

Epilogue

Henry Ford said that "Anyone who keeps learning stays young." If so, then I must be ten years younger than when I started this project! It has been an amazing journey spanning many years and many miles, and I'm grateful for every minute and inch of it.

It isn't every day in this world of information overload that one gets the chance to make new discoveries, but I've learned so much, and each revelation made me hungry for the next. I hope I have been able to convey that spirit of adventure in the pages of this book.

From all I have personally seen and experienced, I have no doubt that the landscape of the Hudson Valley and northern New Jersey was once filled with stone calendar and ceremonial sites, most likely built by Native Americans. With so much destruction and development, we are very fortunate that some of these sites survived—and there still may be even more that are unknown or unrecognized.

It is my heartfelt wish that this book will open some eyes and spark some curiosity and enthusiasm. I urge you to be a voice for these forgotten or overlooked sites. Tell your local historians, teachers, and politicians to help bring awareness to what just might be the Hudson Valley's greatest treasures, so that they may be preserved for future generations.

I have no doubt that I have only scratched the surface of what is to be learned, but I am equally confident that there is sound and reasonable evidence for historians, archaeologists, and astronomers to move forward and study the stone chambers, cairns, walls, perched boulders, and standing stones.

There *are* mysteries in the Hudson Valley, but sometimes, mysteries can be solved.

Linda Zimmermann
March 2016

INDEX

www.ingramcontent.com/pod-product-compliance
Lightning Source LLC
Chambersburg PA
CBHW020856090426
42736CB00008B/399